# The I Ching Workbook

# The I CHING Workbook

A Step-by-Step Guide to Learning the Wisdom of the Oracles

## ROGER GREEN

THUNDER BAY
P·R·E·S·S

SAN DIEGO, CALIFORNIA

**Thunder Bay Press**
An imprint of the Advantage Publishers Group
THUNDER BAY 5880 Oberlin Drive, San Diego, CA 92121-4794
P · R · E · S · S www.thunderbaybooks.com

Text: Roger Green
Additional text: Antonia Beattie

All notations of errors or omissions should be addressed to Thunder Bay Press, Editorial Department, at the above address. All other correspondence (author inquiries, permissions) concerning the content of this book should be addressed to Lansdowne Publishing, Level 1, 18 Argyle Street, The Rocks NSW 2000, Australia.

ISBN 1-59223-044-X

Set in Stone Sans and Goudy on QuarkXPress
Printed in China

1  2  3  4  5     08  07  06  05  04

*Thanks to Marise L. Hamm for her editorial assistance.*

*The aim of I Ching practice is to bring about balance in which celestial consciousness guides earthly awareness to follow the rhythm of nature.*

# CONTENTS

**INTRODUCTION:  8**
The classic book of Eastern philosophy
Origins
Patterns of energy
A universal message
About this book

**CHAPTER ONE:**
**KEY CONCEPTS OF THE I CHING 16**
Universal energy: qi
Yin and yang
Building blocks of the I Ching
Origins of the trigram concept
The eight trigrams
The hexagrams

**CHAPTER TWO:**
**CONSULTING THE I CHING 32**
Honoring the I Ching
Clearing your mind
Preparing your space
Preparing yourself
Knowing what to ask
An I Ching ritual

**CHAPTER THREE:**
**THE EIGHT TRIGRAMS 44**
Key to the trigrams
Heaven
Earth
Thunder
Wind
Water
Fire
Mountain
Lake
Trigrams and social interactions

**CHAPTER FOUR:**
**HOW TO CONSTRUCT A HEXAGRAM 80**
Methods of casting
The coins
Coin-casting method
Bead-casting method
Identifying your hexagram
Interpreting the hexagrams

**CHAPTER FIVE:**
**ADVANCED HEXAGRAM READINGS 90**
Changing lines
The position and meaning of the
    changing line
The progressed hexagram
Nuclear hexagrams

**CHAPTER SIX:**
**THE SIXTY-FOUR HEXAGRAMS OF THE**
**I CHING 104**
Strategy for reading the hexagrams
Interpreting the answer
Guide to the hexagrams
Hexagrams 1–64
Your reflections on the I Ching

**CHAPTER SEVEN:**
**OUR INTERACTION WITH THE SPIRITUAL 178**
How to use you lucky ming gua number

**FURTHER READING 184**
**ANSWERS TO WORKBOOK EXERCISES 184**
**GLOSSARY 185**
**INDEX 188**
**QUICK REFERENCE GUIDE 192**

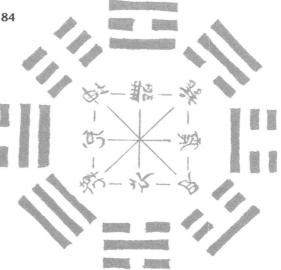

# INTRODUCTION

## THE CLASSIC BOOK OF EASTERN PHILOSOPHY

The *I Ching\** is a spiritual treasure. It is one of the most prized books of ancient Chinese literature. It is lyrical and inspirational; its wisdom can transform those who consult it. According to tradition, it has its origins in the most ancient practice of divination. The I Ching (pronounced "Yi Jing") translates literally as "Classic of Change"; the "I" means changes in the flow of life energy and "Ching" means classic. It is also known as the Book of Changes and is perhaps the oldest writing on philosophy, cosmology, divination, and self-transformation in Chinese civilization. The I Ching has often been called the philosophical backbone to traditional Chinese medicine, Eastern cosmology and astrology, *feng shui*, and tai chi chuan. It is one of very few books consistently to have escaped intentional destruction from the first Chin emperor in the third century B.C. to Mao Tse-tung in the twentieth century.

The I Ching makes predictions for every individual based on the theory that the earth is manifested from the *Universal Creative Order*—the principle of order in nature that describes the dualities, or rhythm of life, as evolving from oneness. There are sixty-four basic units of divination, the *hexagrams*, which represent the sum of the forces acting on earth, heaven, and humanity at any one moment. The hexagrams are illustrations of archetypal experiences.

One of the most fascinating aspects of Chinese *Taoist* philosophy highlighted by the I Ching is the interrelationship that occurs between many aspects of life we normally do not associate with one another. Everything that exists is meaningfully related, as it is believed that everything in the universe is of "one piece."

*Terms described in the glossary (pages 185–187) are highlighted in **bold italics** the first time they are used.

# ORIGINS

The I Ching is the essence of Chinese Taoist philosophy, conceived some 6,000 years ago. It seems highly likely that the I Ching text arose from pieces of oral wisdom, which were collected and eventually written down, rounded, and polished over time to give a sense of unity and purpose.

Just as the Pentateuch was originally attributed to the great leader Moses, the I Ching has been attributed to the great leaders of Chinese history, such as Fu Xi (Fu Hsi), a legendary emperor and sage, Emperor Wen Wang, and the Duke of Chou. The I Ching developed during the Chou dynasty and is sometimes known as the "Chou I"—it was during this time that Emperor Wen Wang, founder of the Chou dynasty, rearranged the sixty-four basic units of divination and wrote judgments or commentaries on each hexagram. His son, the Duke of Chou, added commentaries on each line of each hexagram and developed the concept of *changing lines* that you will read about in this book.

Like many national epics, the authorship of the I Ching belongs to the community of the early Chinese people. It is not only the product of Chinese history; it has also become an intrinsic aspect of the Chinese people and has been the source of inspiration for Far Eastern people for many centuries.

The I Ching has played a strong role in shaping the arts of alchemy and medicine. These are products of centuries of experimentation, research, and development and are also part of the *Shenmiwenhua* ("Mysterious Culture") of China—those with an interest in the magical, mystical, and the miraculous. The I Ching is considered part of the eight "rays" of traditional Chinese medicine—acupuncture, herbal medicine, *chi* exercise (martial arts and qi gong, for example), food energetics, heat application, meditation, astrology, and feng shui. It is the magnum opus of Eastern metaphysics.

# PATTERNS OF ENERGY

The I Ching contains a wealth of Taoist knowledge and reveals the pattern and pulse of life. Taoism, along with Confucianism and Buddhism, is one of the three great philosophies of China. "Tao" can be translated as "path." The I Ching contains the Taoist notions of oneness and that everything in the universe is part of a continuum. The ancient Taoist sages mapped out the nature of a "real" human being and developed a language to explain its mechanism. The I Ching is the result of these investigations into the nature of reality.

The concepts of *synchronicity* (a word coined by Carl Jung from his study of the I Ching) and what is called *ying*, or resonance, underlie the I Ching. One of the principal assumptions behind the I Ching is that everything that happens is meaningfully related. Everything that arises in one moment shares the significance of that moment. Events occur not only simultaneously but also in a meaningful interrelationship. Everything in the phenomenal universe is related, part of the pattern in the universe at that point in time.

Essentially, the I Ching identifies patterns of universal energy at work within the world. It reflects the belief that the world is in a state of ceaseless flux or change. Everything is constantly evolving, being born, growing, reaching maturity, decaying, and dying. The world is always changing, in complex but orderly and rhythmic patterns.

The I Ching descriptions of these patterns are couched in a highly symbolic, allusive, and evocative language that points to the synchronicity of all things. The world as envisaged by the I Ching is like a web of numerous strands, organically and synchronically intertwined without clear-cut cause-and-effect relationships.

*There is something obscure which is complete*
*Before Heaven and Earth arose:*
*Tranquil, quiet, standing alone without change,*
*Moving around without peril.*
**Lao Tsu**, a famous Taoist sage (604–531 B.C.)
Tao Te Ching

# A UNIVERSAL MESSAGE

When you work with the I Ching, it will quickly become apparent that its wisdom is universal and can be used independently of the context of Chinese culture. Despite its antiquity, the I Ching remains fully relevant to the modern world and has amazed generations concerning the relevance of its answers. It is like a trusted friend who will always give honest feedback. It offers guidance in everyday life and helps one to determine favorable actions and avoid misconduct.

The I Ching is an oracle through which we can receive information from the spiritual worlds. It is a divinatory tool as well as an instrument to develop intuition and perception, a guide for self-reflection, and a source of inexhaustible inspiration. Tuning in to the I Ching elevates your mind, helping you connect with higher spheres of wisdom from which you receive philosophical answers beyond the understanding of the rational mind.

The I Ching is a collection of symbols and archetypes and is an introduction into a way of symbolic thinking. It is essentially practical. It makes you ask questions and work at deciphering symbols in order to find your answers. It helps you make sense of things, explore your inner truth, and connect with your life's purpose.

The aim of the I Ching is to help you become a real human being, rather than a vacillating product of social and cultural accident—to be fully awake, autonomous, and capable of making change and exercising free will. The I Ching is based on observations of nature and human life, the interaction of universal laws and individual behavior. It emphasizes positive change as its central concept in development of the realized individual.

It raises the hidden tendencies of the human mind into the light of conscious awareness in order to give us a glimpse of the possibilities before us and a chance to choose the best course of action. It helps us to make the best of our lives and to live in harmony with prevailing circumstances, whatever they may be.

## ABOUT THIS BOOK

The I Ching is a complex divination system. It combines a universal philosophy with practical advice. When you are able to read its messages, you can apply them for greater understanding of many aspects of your life. But to read these messages you will first need to understand the various units of meaning in the I Ching system. This workbook takes you through these units step by step. These steps outline the structure of this workbook.

At all stages you will be given exercises to help you develop your skill at understanding and using the I Ching. These exercises will also help you to understand the universality of the I Ching—how it can speak to you personally and enable you to understand your own part in a world where everything—human, natural, physical, spiritual, and divine—is linked.

**Step 1 Learn about the energy concept.** In Chinese Taoist philosophy, there is an energy, **qi**, that flows through all things. Qi is generated by the interaction between **yin and yang**, two opposite forms of energy. In diagram form, yin is shown as a broken line and yang as a solid line (pages 18–19).

**Step 2 Understand combinations of energy.** It was believed that after the Ultimate Beginning of the universe, the two primary powers of yin and yang interacted. Four different energy combinations were produced. Each was represented as a diagram with two lines, broken for yin and solid for yang. The top line represented heaven and the bottom, earth (pages 25–27).

**Step 3 Add the human element.** Later, a center line was added to each to represent humanity, poised between heaven and earth. The three-line figure is known as a **trigram** and is the basic unit of meaning of the I Ching (pages 25–27).

**Step 4 Study the trigrams.** There are eight trigrams, formed from all possible combinations of yin and yang lines. Each has been associated with a basic element that reflects the quality of its energy: Heaven, Earth, Thunder, Wind, Water, Fire, Mountain, and Lake. Each has a symbolic meaning and depicts physical, psychological, natural, and social manifestations (pages 44–79).

**Step 5 Explore the hexagram concept.** In the I Ching, the trigrams have been combined in pairs to form hexagrams, six-line figures. There are sixty-four hexagrams. They form the text of the I Ching. Each hexagram is associated with a judgment, or evaluation. It has several layers of symbolic meaning (pages 28–31 and 104–177).

**Step 6 Consult the I Ching.** In the I Ching divination system, the person seeking enlightenment from the wisdom of the I Ching needs to choose a hexagram and then read it to see how it relates to his or her quest (see steps 7 to 12). The process of finding the relevant hexagram is quite complex, but the rewards are great (pages 32–36).

**Step 7 Ask a question.** The seeker begins by framing a question that the I Ching will answer (pages 37–41).

**Step 8 Cast for a reply.** Then coins or beads are used by the seeker to begin casting for an answer. From the casting process, six yin and/or yang lines are produced (pages 80–89).

**Step 9 Construct a hexagram.** These lines will form one of the sixty-four hexagrams. A table is consulted to find the number of the hexagram that has been produced (pages 80–89).

**Step 10 Read the hexagram.** The seeker reads the relevant hexagram and relates its message to his or her question (pages 88 and 104–107).

**Step 11 Construct another hexagram.** Some original hexagrams can be altered to form another hexagram. The seeker can find the number of this hexagram and consult it. It will give more information on the same issue (pages 90–103).

**Step 12 Look at the nuclear hexagram.** The original hexagram can be altered to form a nuclear hexagram, giving its hidden meaning. The seeker can find the number of the hexagram and read about its meaning (pages 98–103).

**Step 13 Reflect.** Chapter Six lists some thoughts relating to each of the hexagrams. Use these thoughts to reflect on the hexagram's meaning and on the universal messages of the I Ching (pages 174–177).

## CREATING YOUR I CHING JOURNAL

*I Ching Journal*

Date
Location
Situation

Exercises/readings

Insights

You will need to create an I Ching journal to accompany your journey throughout this workbook. Buy a new book with blank pages. Choose carefully; the journal should appear inviting to you, as it will be sharing your innermost thoughts and questions. Find a clean piece of cloth to wrap the journal in so that you can keep it safe and private. Again, choose a cloth that appeals to you. Put some thought into selecting the color and texture.

Use this journal to record the questions you formulate and the answers you receive during your consultations with the I Ching. Record the actual events that happen at the time, writing as complete an account as you can of your emotional, physical, intellectual, and spiritual life at that time.

Remember to log in the date, location, and situation. Record also your response to all of the workbook exercises in this book.

As time goes by, consult the journal. You will be fascinated by your thoughts and by the answers that have come to you. Read this journal again many years from now. You may find that the questions formulated previously are useful for considering issues in your life at a different time.

Once you have worked through pages 37 to 41 on formulating questions to ask the I Ching, use your journal to record your first attempts at questions. Rewrite the question in your journal as often as you need to. Later, use this record to help you with simplifying other questions and reducing them to the issue most significant to you.

Also, write down your own interpretations of the I Ching's answer and what actions you think you will need to take or avoid in order to make use of the wisdom of the answer. As you write, reflect on your willingness to know more about your current situation. The more you cultivate a willingness to understand your own life and the world around you, the more your mind will develop.

## SPELLING OF NAMES

There are variant names in English for aspects of the I Ching such as the hexagrams and the trigrams. These variants have arisen because the original terms had to be transliterated from the Chinese characters into our own alphabet. In this workbook, the most recently accepted translations have been used, with alternative spellings given in parentheses where relevant—for example, Qian (Ch'ien).

*The I Ching develops a sense of the real essence of the mind, which means a mind that is keen, incorruptible, decisive, detached, independent, consistent, dedicated, objective, self-controlled, humble, sincere, tolerant, free from compulsive thinking, and content.*

## CHAPTER ONE

# KEY CONCEPTS OF THE I CHING

*Discover the history and philosophy of the I Ching. Learn about universal energy, yin and yang, the trigrams, and the hexagrams.*

## UNIVERSAL ENERGY: QI

Understanding the basic concepts of interactions of energy is fundamental to developing an appreciation of the I Ching. While various cultures are concerned with the interaction of energies, the concept has found its most sophisticated and organized expression in the I Ching.

There is an intangible, invisible, but powerful energy that flows through everything in the universe. In Chinese Taoist philosophy, the energy flow is called qi, chi, or ki (pronounced "chee") and there are various types or "qualities" of qi, such as heaven qi, earth qi, human qi, personal qi, and kidney qi. Qi encompasses all material and nonmaterial phenomena in creation. It is a universal state, existing everywhere.

Qi is believed to be a combination of energies generated by the shifting balances and tensions between the earth and the cosmos. It can be broadly defined as the movement of nontangible energy or vibrations between the two primary poles in the universe, the yin and yang energies. Yin is a passive, flexible energy, while yang is an active, firm (solid) energy.

While qi is understood to be a flow of energy, it is also described in terms of its "quality." Emotions, intellect, atmosphere, temperature, physical traits, sensory stimulations, and colors are all described in terms of their quality of qi or their particular balance of yin or yang.

Heaven qi is the energy of the cosmos and the movement of the clouds and wind above the earth. Earth qi is the energy generated by the shape of the earth, the force of its magnetic fields, and the effect of the combination of the five Chinese *elements*—Earth,

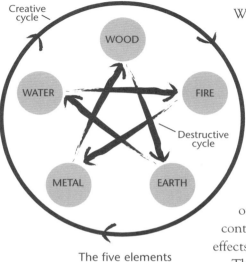

The five elements

Wood, Fire, Metal, and Water. Human qi is the energy generated in the social interactions between people. The trinity of heaven, earth, and humanity, often referred to as the Chinese trinity, underlies the divination process in the I Ching. There are more intimate levels of qi, such as personal qi, which reflects the energy that moves through the body, thoughts, emotions, and personality. Every organ in the body has its particular quality of qi. Qi is considered to be our life essence. Our physical bodies are fields of continually moving energy (these pathways and effects are studied in acupuncture).

The I Ching sees the need for each human to experience individually the relationships between life's energies. This is fundamental to what can be called the spiritual approach to life. It is this perception of energetic reality that brings mystery and delight to our everyday experiences. This kind of understanding brings a broadening of vision and a more open approach to life and its circumstances. We start to see the connection of mind and body, life and death, summer and winter, and the rational and intuitive sides of everything. It is with this receptiveness that we need to approach working with the I Ching.

*The Great Way is not difficult for those who have no preferences. When love and hate are both absent, everything becomes clear and undisguised. Make the smallest distinction, however, and heaven and earth are set infinitely apart. If you wish to see the truth then hold no opinions for or against. The struggle of what one likes and dislikes is the disease of the mind.*
THE BOOK OF TRUE FAITH BY THE MASTER SOSAN

## YIN AND YANG

In Chinese Taoist philosophy, the life force, qi, fluctuates between and is stimulated by the interaction between the two opposing forces of yin and yang. Yin and yang are the great primordial forces of nature. They are complementary and antagonistic forces and form a constant cycle of regeneration and degeneration. They govern the cycle of birth, growth, and decay of all things material, mental, and spiritual. This regular alternation between the energies of yin and yang is the fundamental process of existence.

Even the phenomenal world, according to Chinese Taoist philosophy, was created through the interaction of yin and yang. The yang state of *tai chi*, or the Great Ultimate, arose spontaneously from the yin *wu chi*, or Ultimate Nothingness.

## A BALANCED COMBINATION

Yin and yang are not precisely defined, but at their most basic level yin corresponds with female, passive energy and flexibility, while yang corresponds with male, aggressive energy and firmness of will. The correct blending of yin and yang is considered important for both social and spiritual life.

The complete or real human being is considered to be a balanced combination of two levels of experience. We maintain contact with the higher, vaster dimension of nirvana, or enlightened experience of consciousness, while at the same time we live in the earthly domain. This is one meaning of the blending or uniting of the yin and yang and is expressed in the Taoist phrase, "Being beyond the world while living in the world."

The principle of yin and yang, as explained in the I Ching, is often called the philosophical backbone to traditional Chinese medicines such as acupuncture, environmental studies such as feng shui, and Eastern astrology.

*Let yourself and your attention be fluid. Follow the movement.*

## A STUDY OF CHANGE

Essentially, the I Ching is the study of change, which the ancient Chinese reduced to the simplest of concepts—yin and yang. For thousands of years, humankind has been discussing the ins and outs of change. In order to achieve a degree of mental harmony, we have sought to understand change itself. This prevents us from being rigid and fixed so that we might flow with change rather than unwittingly oppose it. In Chinese Taoist philosophy, change is the process of yin transforming into yang and yang transforming into yin. Patterns of change are nothing more than combinations of yin and yang in the process of transformation.

In the I Ching, yin is symbolized as a broken line and yang by a solid line. In the original texts, these were spoken of as firm, light lines (yang) or dark, yielding lines (yin). An open circle indicated yang while a solid dark circle represented yin.

|      |      |
|:----:|:----:|
| ——  —— | ———— |
| Yin | Yang |

This could be called the binary hardware operating system of the universe. There is no symbolism more condensed than a broken/solid line. The concept appears in our simplest gadgetry, such as the "on/off" switch, to our most complex modern computer operating systems.

| Yang | Yin |
|------|-----|
| Solid line | Broken line |
| Heaven | Earth |
| Masculine principle | Feminine principle |
| Activity | Passivity |
| Movement | Stillness |
| Heat | Cold |
| Exterior | Interior |
| Outward | Inward |

| Yang | Yin |
| --- | --- |
| Up | Down |
| Full energy | Hidden potential energy |
| Light | Dark |
| Warmth | Coldness |
| Dryness | Wetness |
| Hardness | Softness |
| Aggression | Yielding |
| Odd numbers | Even numbers |
| Summer | Winter |
| Youth | Old age |
| Increase | Decrease |

It is helpful to think of the I Ching as a language of change and continuous movement. The inhalation and exhalation of your body can be thought of as a microcosm of the expansion and contraction of the universe. We are an energetic and vibrational manifestation of the entire cosmos, and as such, we are subject to the endless changes. Learning this language will do two things for you: it will strengthen and refine your willingness to make change and it will show you what is going on in your life. After some study, it will become an invaluable tool in your life.

Qi flows auspiciously around potted plants, particularly those with rounded leaves. In a large, sparsely furnished room, the energy may feel unbalanced by too much yin (space) dominating too little yang (furniture). The energy would feel dissipated and flat. In a small, crowded room, the energy may feel unbalanced by too little yin (space) dominated by too much yang (furniture). The energy would feel too suppressed and unsettled. In a dark room the energy may feel overly yin (passive).

**WORKBOOK EXERCISES**

1. The following exercise will help you identify the quality of energy flowing through your body. Try to figure out which of the following organs have a yin or yang quality of energy. Dense and compact organs are yin while yang organs are hollow and long. For example, the liver is yin and the gallbladder is yang. Write your answers in your journal.
   - Heart
   - Small intestine
   - Spleen
   - Stomach
   - Lungs
   - Large intestine
   - Kidneys
   - Bladder

   *See page 184 for answers.*

2. You can also find the effects of yin and yang energy in your outer environment. In your I Ching journal, list the yin and yang qualities in your working environment and your home environment. For example:
   - Where is energy fast-moving?
   - Where is energy still?
   - Where is it light?
   - Where is it dark?
   - Where is there moisture?
   - Where is there noise?

   Corners create fast-moving qi that feels uncomfortable and is considered inauspicious.

## BUILDING BLOCKS OF THE I CHING

The I Ching is formally attributed to Fu Xi (Fu Hsi) (2953–2838 B.C.), one of the great legendary emperors in China and one of the most important figures in Chinese cultural mythology. It is believed that he formulated the concept of the trigrams, or **gua**, the building blocks of the I Ching, as a philosophical and divinatory system. These trigrams were revealed to Fu Xi on the back of a tortoise.

There is archaeological evidence that about 4,000 years ago, people in Mongolia, Tibet, China, India, and other parts of the world heated the shells of tortoises with red-hot pokers and used the resulting crack patterns to foretell the future. This is known as **plastromancy**. It was believed that the tortoise possessed this mysterious oracular power because it survived longer than other living beings.

In Chinese beliefs, the tortoise's shell is a symbol of long life and happiness—the shell is also believed to be the home of divinity. Fu Xi was taken by the unusual black-and-white markings on the shell, which he saw as a sign from heaven. He directed his scholars to use the shell as a focal point to organize and develop ideas that would incorporate their experiences, observations, and knowledge.

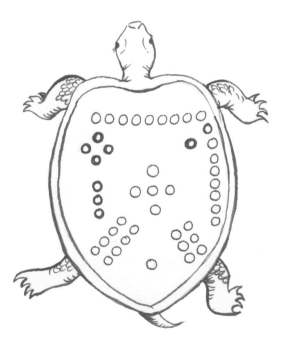

The markings revealed a surprising symmetry. The shell looked like a square divided into nine equal segments, three across and three down. Each square contained an arrangement of a number of dots from one to nine. The sum of the numbers across, up, down, and diagonally equaled the same number—15.

| 4 | 9 | 2 |
|---|---|---|
| 3 | 5 | 7 |
| 8 | 1 | 6 |

As can be seen from the illustration, the central square corresponds to the number 5. This arrangement is called the Lo Shu or the Magic Square.

## ELEMENTS AND NUMBERS

| 4 | 9 | 2 |
|---|---|---|
| Wood | Fire | Earth |
| 3 | 5 | 7 |
| Wood | Earth | Metal |
| 8 | 1 | 6 |
| Earth | Water | Metal |

The Magic Square

In Fu Xi's configuration of the shell design, the central number, 5, symbolizes the earth and the number of elements or forces of nature that are in a constant state of movement. It is believed that everything on earth, including human beings, are made up of a combination of the five elements of Metal, Water, Wood, Fire, and Earth.

Fu Xi considered the balanced placement of the nine numbers to be divinely inspired. The central square within the nine-grid square represented the balance of earth and heaven, while each of the eight squares surrounding it corresponded to one of the eight great manifestations of natural energy.

The configuration of eight squares and their corresponding numbers is known as the Universal Chart, representing the universe and life. It is also known as the **bagua**. The arrangement of the trigrams differed before and after the Han dynasty (206 B.C.–220 A.D.). Before this time the squares were arranged in the Early Heaven Sequence, while the Later Heaven Sequence was used after this time. The Later Heaven Sequence is the one most used in modern times, especially in the practice of feng shui.

Later Heaven Sequence

## ORIGINS OF THE TRIGRAM CONCEPT

In ancient Chinese cosmology, after the Ultimate Beginning, the two primary energies of heaven (yang) and earth (yin) were created (see pages 18–20). It was believed that when these two primary powers interacted they produced four complex combinations of energy.

Each combination was symbolized by two lines—solid for yang and broken for yin:

Great yang      Lesser yang      Lesser yin      Great yin

These combinations of energy indicated the interrelationships between heaven and earth. The top line in each combination was the heaven line and the bottom line the earth line.

Then a third line was inserted for each combination. This ensured that the trinity principle of cosmic unity, or the three treasures of heaven, earth, and humanity (**san cai**), was attained. This line was inserted in the middle of each combination as the center line, representing humanity. The result was eight three-line combinations, or trigrams. Each represented one of the outer squares on the shell as seen by Fu Xi. At one end of the spectrum, the trigram with three broken lines represented great yin, and at the other the trigram with three solid lines represented great yang. There are eight trigrams, as this is the total number of possible combinations of yin and yang lines, as illustrated below.

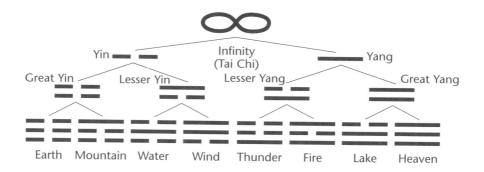

The trinity of heaven, earth, and humanity.
The trigrams represent our reality as the human standing between heaven and earth.

*"One produces two; two produces three; three is manifested as all possible things."*
Lao Tsu, TAO TE CHING

Each of these trigrams was associated with a basic element that reflected the quality of its energy: Heaven, Earth, Thunder, Wind, Water, Fire, Mountain, and Lake. The table below outlines the major aspects of these eight trigrams. The eight trigrams were believed to unveil the heavenly processes in nature and to aid in the understanding of the character of everything—they could be used to depict and explain the existence of all physical, psychological, natural, and social manifestations. Fu Xi called the pattern of interaction between these eight trigrams the Laws of Change or the Principles of the Universe.

## THE EIGHT TRIGRAMS

The eight trigrams, each consisting of differing combinations of three solid and/or broken lines, are associated with various aspects and elements of the world, and each is traditionally called by a specific name and associated with distinctive symbolic connotations, correspondences, or resonances. In particular, each trigram corresponds with the name of a natural phenomenon that reflects the particular trigram's energetic quality, such as Heaven, Earth, Mountain, or Fire. This table outlines important aspects of each trigram (see Chapter Three, pages 44–79).

| Trigram name (English) | Trigram name (Chinese) | Trigram symbol | Symbolic aspect | Associated shape |
|---|---|---|---|---|
| Heaven | Qian | ☰ | The Initiating | ○ |
| Earth | Kun | ☷ | The Responding | □ |
| Thunder | Zhen | ☳ | The Arousing | ∪ |
| Wind | Xun | ☴ | The Penetrating | 〒 |
| Water | Kan | ☵ | The Cautious | ▽ |
| Fire | Li | ☲ | The Clinging | △ |
| Mountain | Gen | ☶ | The Stillness | ∩ |
| Lake | Dui | ☱ | The Joyous | ⋁ |

# THE HEXAGRAMS

The text of the I Ching is divided into sixty-four chapters, each corresponding to one hexagram. The word is derived from the Greek *hexa* ("six") and *gramma* ("something written"). Each hexagram is composed on the basis of a specific spiritual principle.

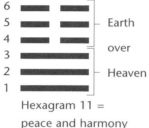

6
5
4 — Earth
3 — over
2
1 — Heaven

Hexagram 11 = peace and harmony

A hexagram is a set of six lines, made up of two trigrams. The lower or bottom trigram indicates the cause of the situation and also relates to what is happening in the mundane world. The upper or top trigram signifies the surface appearances of the issue and also relates to what is happening in the celestial world.

The complete cycle of the eight phases of yin and yang. This diagram illustrates how the eight trigrams combine to make the sixty-four hexagrams based on the Early Heaven Sequence.

## WHAT THE HEXAGRAMS TELL US

In the text of the I Ching, each hexagram is associated with a judgment, or evaluation, along with an image and complementary information related to each line. The I Ching's distinctive style is that of short sentences, which give a minimum of information and leave the reader to use his or her own understanding to fit it into a specific context. For example, see hexagram 11 (page 120). This is one of the most favorable hexagrams and is called "Peace." The judgment for this hexagram speaks of the departure of the small and of the coming of the great, predicting good fortune and success. The image is that of the union of the sky and the earth. To help you become familiar with the principles of the sixty-four hexagrams, see pages 110–173 for a summary of what each hexagram means.

## ORIGINS OF THE HEXAGRAMS

It is unclear who developed the sixty-four hexagrams from the eight trigrams. Early traditions attribute authorship to Fu Xi or Emperor Wen, founder of the Chou dynasty. It is possible that Fu Xi was responsible for the creation of hexagrams. It is generally believed that different arrangements of hexagrams had existed before Emperor Wen rearranged them during the Chou dynasty into the present form. Emperor Wen is also believed to have been responsible for the appended judgments (*Kua T'uan*). The *Ta Chuan* ("Great Commentary") also gives some evidence to support this idea.

The writing of the judgments occurred during a time when there was great unrest in the land and fighting between Emperor Wen and the tyrant Chou Hsin. Emperor Wen was imprisoned for seven years. It is traditionally believed that the emperor, a great diviner, whiled the days of his imprisonment working on the arrangement of the hexagrams and writing the commentaries on the sixty-four hexagrams of the I Ching. According to tradition, each hexagram appeared in order on the wall of the prison as a vision, giving some credence to the thought that the present arrangement of hexagrams and appended judgments are more than the mere product of human wisdom—they are revelations of higher reality. It is interesting that the judgments of the I Ching often warn against danger and unrest. They could be a reflection of that turbulent time.

## USING THE HEXAGRAMS

The set of hexagrams can be used as an oracle. To approach the hexagrams with this purpose in mind, the following steps should be taken:

1. **Ask a question mentally**. For ways to ask the right kind of question and to prepare to tap into the wisdom of the I Ching, see Chapter Two.
2. **Use coins or beads to cast for a reply**. Using coins or beads as you think about your question (see pages 80–87), you can get a response consisting of six yin and/or yang lines.
3. **Construct a hexagram from these lines** (see page 88). This will represent the answer to your question.
4. **Begin interpreting the answer** by looking for the number of the hexagram you have constructed (see the table on page 192).
5. **Find the description of your hexagram** in Chapter Six, where the key to each hexagram is given. The hexagrams are presented in numerical order.

The hexagram will:
• show you the state of play between the universe and yourself.
• help you understand your situation.
• give you an indication of the path that you will need to tread to achieve your goal.

## THE THREE TYPES OF HEXAGRAMS

You will learn about three types of hexagrams in this workbook:
• The **ben gua**, which is the first, or original, hexagram, which is constructed in response to a question put to the I Ching.
• The **zhi gua**, a **progressed hexagram**, which is constructed if the first, or original, hexagram contains changing lines (see pages 90–97). This will give you further information about your situation and could represent your immediate future.
• A **hu gua**, or **nuclear hexagram**, which is constructed of two trigrams made from the middle four lines of the first, or original, hexagram (see pages 98–102). This will give you further insight into the deeper meanings of the situation.

**WORKBOOK EXERCISES**

1. Exercise your powers of intuition as you begin to learn about the hexagrams. Look at Chapter Six, which provides a key for all sixty-four of the hexagrams. Flick through the pages until you come upon a hexagram that looks appealing to you. Read its message. Now answer these questions in your I Ching journal.
   - Does the message of the hexagram reflect your current situation in life? If so, describe the similarities between the message and your situation.
   - Is it a state you wish to achieve?
   - Does it present you with a challenge?
   - Why do you think this hexagram appeals to you?
   - Are you overcoming obstacles or are you on a progressive path?

2. Now go back through Chapter Six and familiarize yourself with the shape, names, and meanings of all sixty-four hexagrams. As you do this, write down any interesting thoughts or insights you may have in your I Ching journal.

The Early Heaven Sequence

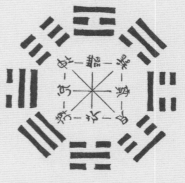

The Later Heaven Sequence

## CHAPTER TWO

# CONSULTING THE I CHING

*Learn how to consult the I Ching. How to honor the oracle, clear your mind, and prepare yourself and your space. What questions should you ask?*

Chinese Taoist philosophy tells us that in our actions, our thoughts, and our dreams, we exist in the same universe as everything outside of ourselves. There is a synchronistic sympathy between us and this world. Both the microcosm of the individual and the macrocosm of the universe exist simultaneously, obey all the same rules, and have a common origin. There is a relationship between all things regardless of how large or small they are. When we consult the I Ching, we are entering into a relationship with the cyclical movement of energy as it exists at that point in time and space. We are tapping into the energy of the universe that mirrors the pattern of energy in our own lives.

When we seek the wisdom of the I Ching, we obtain a reflection of what we know intuitively. We are seeking the wisdom that is hidden in our own lives.

Consulting the I Ching will help us to:
- sharpen our intuition
- cultivate a meditative quality in our lives
- become watchful, anticipating the problems that will arise through our path in life
- remain unattached when problems do arise
- choose a pathway through life, making decisions about business, relationships, career, and health
- gain some hints about our future or fate

# HONORING THE I CHING

To use the I Ching as a valuable tool for understanding yourself and your world, you will first need to learn how to approach it correctly. Doing so is both a technique and an art. In time and with the correct tools, you will become skilled at using the I Ching for your personal enlightenment. This workbook offers you some tools for developing your technique.

The fundamental principle is this: if you want the I Ching to answer you, let it hear you clearly. Approach it with a sincere heart and ask a question that expresses simply and without confusion the issue that is absorbing you. Then the I Ching will receive you.

Clear your mind first of other worries or interests. The less the mind is caught up in everyday concerns and agitating thoughts, the easier it will be for you to tap into the wisdom of the spirit world. This book will help you to use meditation and other practices to clear your mind and create open lines of communication with the wisdom of the I Ching.

## THE BENEFITS OF CONSULTING THE I CHING

The I Ching speaks to everyone. It is the voice of ancient sages who have incorporated thousands of years of astute observations into the work. Its wisdom is universal.

By taking appropriate action after consultation with the I Ching, you may be able to determine your own destiny. Whatever you want to know, the I Ching will help, especially if your intentions are ethically sound and you are willing to accept whatever answer is given. Set aside your fears and desires and take up the challenge of what the I Ching tells you. Be brave.

On occasion your intuition may be strong and you may be totally confident about making difficult decisions. However, you may still benefit from consulting the I Ching. It will further your understanding and appreciation of the people and events in your life. And it will also allow you to become more aware of the universal truths that underlie your own life and the lives of all other beings and natural things.

# CLEARING YOUR MIND

Here is a useful technique for preparing yourself to address the I Ching. It is a meditation that will clear your mind of small concerns and make you open to the wisdom that will follow. On the following pages, you will also learn how to clear your space for this same purpose.

## MAKING A SMALL ALTAR

You may also consider making a small altar to honor the spiritual within you and the world. In your selected area, place a small table or cloth on the floor. Arrange three small bowls in the center of the table or cloth. Then do the following:

1. Spoon some cooked brown rice into the central bowl. This bowl represents the infinite.
2. Pour a small amount of spring water into the bowl on your left. This symbolizes yin energy.
3. Into the bowl on your right, pour some sea salt to symbolize yang energy.
4. Decorate your altar with an attractive assortment of small rocks and flowers that you have found around your home.

# MEDITATION

Try the following meditation before consulting the I Ching. Find a place where you will not be disturbed and sit comfortably.

Now read this text. Speak each line separately. Imagine that you are following the directions of each line:

*Empty your mind: let go of its contents!*
*Make your mind no mind: get rid of all things!*
*Concentrate your mind: make it unmoving!*
*Pacify your mind: let there be no fear!*
*Make your mind tranquil: keep it from chaos!*
*Straighten your mind: get rid of the crooked!*
*Cleanse your mind: eradicate the foul!*

Once you have done this, imagine that you have now uncovered the following four minds:
• An upright mind: no more reversal.
• A balanced mind: no more highs or lows.
• A luminous mind: no more gloom or darkness.
• A pervasive mind: no more hindrance.

These minds will now shine forth for you. Read their descriptions again, imagining that your mind now incorporates their principles. After some practice, these four minds will begin to radiate naturally. Enjoy the sensation.

# PREPARING YOUR SPACE

In some cultures, sages will often spend much time meditating before attempting some important task. They may also go through a purging process, which may include fasting or eating very lightly, ritual bathing, chanting, or anointing the body with certain oils and fragrances. As you begin your study of the I Ching, you will not need to go quite so far, but rituals for clearing your mind (see page 35) and clearing your space are an effective way of helping you remove the concerns of the everyday world.

It is important to work with the I Ching in a quiet place. Select an area in your home that is not too close to entrances, the hallway, or the bathroom. Turn off the television set and as many electrical appliances as possible. This will help to lower the level of external everyday vibrations around you. To create more distance between yourself and everyday life, light some candles or incense or use some aromatherapy oils to encourage your mind to focus on the spiritual.

# PREPARING YOURSELF

Before consulting the I Ching, empty your mind of your everyday concerns (see page 35). Then sit in a quiet space. If you have set up an I Ching altar according to the instructions on page 34, kneel or sit at your altar.

As you prepare to empty your mind, ensure that your body is comfortable. Sit or kneel. Keep your spine erect. It is imperative that you feel at ease in your body before consulting the I Ching. Feeling at ease physically will:

• improve the quality of your inner life
• allow you to hear and intuit more clearly the messages the I Ching has for you
• heighten your spirituality
• allow you to rest from the worries of the everyday
• bring a sense of healing to your life both physically and spiritually

To help get in touch with a sense of ease, focus on your breathing while sitting or kneeling in front of your altar or in your special space. One useful exercise is to imagine that you are directing your breath directly into the **tantien** (in Chinese culture) or the **hara** (in Japanese culture), located at your abdomen. This is your center of energy. By breathing into and out of this area, it is believed that you are getting into contact with your higher self.

Become your breathing, become your body, become your room, become your dwelling, become your community, become your land, become your planet, become your solar system, become your galaxy, and become your infinite self.

### STIMULATING ENERGY FLOW

Before consulting the I Ching or sitting before your altar, you may wish to do some stretching exercises to stimulate the flow of energy in your body. One such effective exercise is rocking your body. Sit on the floor in a relaxed way with an erect spine. Rock side to side from the hips. Gradually let the range of rocking become smaller and smaller, until you stop. Then rock your head gently from side to side, again allowing it to ease slowly to a standstill.

## KNOWING WHAT TO ASK

What do you want to know when you consult the I Ching? Sometimes you will have to go through a fairly lengthy process before you are clear about the information you need.

### ASKING THE RIGHT QUESTION

- There are right and wrong questions to ask of the I Ching.
- Your choice of question will greatly affect the type of answer you will receive.
- It takes a lot of work with the I Ching in order to master the art of asking correctly formulated questions.
- You may encounter several layers of assumption and confusion before arriving at the question you really want to ask.

## ASKING FROM THE HEART

The questions you ask should come from the heart rather than the head. They need to be related to topics in which you have an emotional involvement. If you ask a question out of intellectual curiosity only, do not expect the I Ching to answer with any clarity. If there is no depth of feeling while you are asking questions, it is likely that there will be no depth of wisdom in the I Ching's answers.

This does not mean that all questions should be serious and philosophical. Some people believe that if we ask questions merely to satisfy our curiosity, the oracle will not answer. What matters is not whether you are curious, but how much your heart is involved in the question. If your curiosity comes from an innocent and sincere place, the answers are likely to be more accurate than you expect. Even if you do not know much about the I Ching, if you ask questions sincerely, it is not rare to receive really significant answers. There is great value in playing with the I Ching in a childlike way, with spontaneity and innocence.

The I Ching answers questions as spiritual masters do. It is not the depth of the questions that attract it to answer, but the depth of your presence. If you are not present in the questions, why should the I Ching be present in the answers?

## WORKBOOK EXERCISES

Give thought to the kinds of questions you have asked in your life:
1. As a small child, what questions did you ask? Listen to young children if you cannot remember. Write down some of the questions that you hear or that come to mind.
2. As a young student at school, what questions were important to you?
3. And now, as an adult?
4. As a child, what questions did you want to ask but were too afraid to do so?
5. As an adult, what questions do you want to ask but are too afraid to do so?

Make note of your thoughts and answers in your I Ching journal.

## SOME USEFUL QUESTIONS

You can ask the I Ching a yes-or-no question, but you will not get a yes-or-no answer, although such answers may be implied. Do not ask overly complex questions. Ask questions about how best to develop yourself and how to communicate with your higher self. Be instinctive about the question. Do not make it conceptual. See the table below for the types of questions you can ask and some examples of these.

| Question type | Examples |
| --- | --- |
| Expects a complete answer | "What can I expect if I travel now?" <br> "What can I expect if I travel later?" |
| Demonstrates that you are in control | "What can I do to increase my earnings this year?" |
| Allows you to balance two outcomes in your mind | "What effect is this new job going to have on my relationship?" <br> "What effect will it have on my relationship if I do not take this new job?" |
| Focuses on special times | "What can I expect on my birthday?" <br> "What do I have to pay attention to in order to be the most productive, loving person in the coming year?" <br> "What does the year have in store for me?" <br> "What can I do to strengthen my marriage?" |
| Describes a state or situation or simply asks for comment | "I think I am falling in love; please comment." <br> "I'm thinking of applying for a new job; please comment." |
| Asks for clarification | "What is going on with my friends?" |

## MORE QUESTIONS TO ASK THE I CHING

You can also ask about:

- Health
- Financial matters
- Social situations
- Business decisions
- Undertakings
- Philosophical issues
- Other people
- Events
- Future conditions
- The past, present, or future
- How to conduct yourself

In every case, the more clearly you can formulate what you actually want to know, the clearer the answer will be.

## STEPS IN FORMULATING QUESTIONS

Write your first attempt at formulating a question in your I Ching journal. Here is an example. Your initial question is, "Shall I leave my job? Shall I take up the offer of a new job?"

1. Ask only one question at a time: "Should I take this new job being offered?"
2. Now take some time to reflect. Inquire deeper into the meaning behind this question.
   "Will I be happy in the new job?"
   "Will I enjoy meeting the people at my new job?"
3. Decide on what you actually want to know.
   "How will I feel about leaving behind the people I like in my present job?"
4. Reflect on, minimize, and clarify the question. Reduce and refine it. Take the time to settle on the optimum wording in order to discover what you really want to know.
   "What is the most important aspect of my work for me?"

5. Say the question out loud before consulting the I Ching.

Some questions can take years to develop. Others will take a much shorter time. Take at least ten minutes to formulate your question.

## ASPECTS OF YOUR QUESTION

Before asking your question, you can also consider which aspect you want answered. In Chinese Taoist philosophy there are three categories, reflecting the three aspects of human experience (see pages 25–27):

| Questions concerning | Aspect they relate to |
| --- | --- |
| Spiritual development | Heaven |
| The body, health, material objects, finances, and the possibility of realizing things on the material plane | Earth |
| Any kind of social circumstances, relationships between people and events, your emotional life | Humanity |

Just as heaven and earth are inextricably linked, with neither more important than the other, so it is that there is no one type of question that is more important that any other. All questions allow us to discover more about essential aspects of ourselves.

## AN I CHING RITUAL

Try the following ritual when sitting before your altar or in your special space. When seated or kneeling comfortably, bow three times in honor of the I Ching trinity of heaven, earth, and humanity. In this way you are expressing your gratitude to creation. When you are ready, simply say anything you wish to communicate to the universe. You may wish to express any current emotions, such as happiness because of a success at work or grief over a lost friend or relative. You may wish to talk with a relative or a friend who has recently passed away or you could even pray for world peace. Do this for three days, at the same time each day, to develop your ability to distance yourself from the mundane world. After the first three days, gradually bring your I Ching tools, such as this workbook, your I Ching journal, and your coins or beads into your special space.

**WORKBOOK EXERCISES**

1. Try all of the exercises below for quieting your mind and preparing yourself to consult the I Ching. Then note in your I Ching journal which are the most effective for you.
   - Find a quiet space where you will be able to consult the I Ching without being disturbed. Spend time there.
   - Set up an altar honoring the basic philosophy of the I Ching—the trinity of heaven, earth, and humanity.
   - Do a series of your favorite stretching exercises or do a gentle rocking exercise to stimulate the flow of energy, or qi, through your body.
   - Practice meditation, allowing your mind to distance itself from everyday concerns.
   - Practice breathing into your abdomen to contact your higher self and begin to feel at ease in your body.
   - Connect in some way with your coins or beads for casting.

2. Establish your own simple ritual to help you tap into the wisdom of the I Ching, using one or more of the suggestions in step 1. You may decide that a combination of these rituals works for you or that you have found a ritual of your own that is effective. Make notes in your I Ching journal.

3. How do you access your sense of being at ease? Do you use music, stretching, cleaning, singing, dancing, meditating, working out in a gym, or working for a charitable organization? Focus on actively feeling at ease and on inspirations you receive about how to make this a permanent state of being. Write notes about your efforts to feel at ease—and your success with these—in your I Ching journal.

4. Write a short paragraph in your I Ching journal about where you find yourself spiritually at this time. Include your thoughts on who you are, the purpose of your life, and how you can involve the study of the I Ching in your spiritual journey.

5. Answer these questions in your I Ching journal. Come back to them when you have been using this workbook for some time.
   - How can I best develop myself?
   - How can I communicate with my higher self?

## CHAPTER THREE

# THE EIGHT TRIGRAMS

*Learn about the eight trigrams—Heaven, Earth, Thunder, Wind, Water, Fire, Mountain, and Lake. What are their special meanings?*

We will now examine in detail the trigrams, the building blocks of the I Ching. As shown earlier, each trigram is composed of three lines of yin and/or yang energy. Each line has a distinctive significance.

## THE THREE TRIGRAM LINES: AN EXPLANATION

| Line | What it represents | Key words |
|------|--------------------|-----------| 
| Top line: Heaven | The sky; everything from the astronomical, heavenly, and cosmological to the climate and current meteorological conditions. Also, the conditions of our spiritual and mental natures. | Astronomy, astrology, moon, stars, cosmic and heavenly qi, time and cycles of change, weather qi, rain, sunlight, heat and cold, wind, the seasons, and the tide. |
| Middle line: Humanity | All that the earth and sky produce and create—natural phenomena (universal and terrestrial) and the emotional and psychological aspects of humanity, social interactions, and exchanges with the environment. | Personal qi, human and social qi, politics, culture, family, neighbors, partners, personality, memories, ideals, visions, sensitivity, and vital qi. |

| Line | What it represents | Key words |
|------|-------------------|-----------|
| Bottom line: Earth | Earth, economics, and the world of materialism and the senses (feeling, smelling, our physical condition). | Topographic qi, landforms, mountains, valleys, rivers, ley lines, environmental qi, dwellings, form and space, color and sound, lighting, furniture and other objects made by human beings. |

There are eight trigrams, as this is the total number of possible combinations of yin and yang lines: Heaven (pages 46–49), Earth (pages 50–53), Thunder (pages 54–57), Wind (pages 58–61), Water (pages 62–65), Fire (pages 66–69), Mountain (pages 70–73), and Lake (pages 74–77).

## KEY TO THE TRIGRAMS

One of the most fascinating aspects of the Chinese Taoist philosophy highlighted by the I Ching is the interrelationship that occurs between many aspects of life that we normally do not associate together. Everything that exists is meaningfully related, as it is believed that everything in the universe is of one piece.

The five Chinese elements, the five senses, the various flavors, animals, seasons, colors, times of day, compass directions, and objects are all believed to be energetically associated with the eight trigrams. This is the Taoist way of thinking, and it is quite different from Western logic. To intuitively interpret the I Ching, it is advisable to open yourself to this Taoist way of thinking.

In this chapter, we will examine each of the eight trigrams and their energetic associations in detail.

*Allow yourself to be open to experiencing the Taoist way of thinking. If you do you will find yourself developing new relationships between yourself and your environment.*

## HEAVEN (QIAN)
### A KEY TO THE HEAVEN TRIGRAM

**People**: Fathers, senior males, men over the age of forty-six, heads of state, leaders, bosses, owners, wise men, emperors and kings, presidents, commanders, monks, saints, hermits, bankers, goldsmiths, and policemen

**Health**: The head and lungs

**Element**: Metal (deep red metal)

**Sense**: Touch

**Flavor**: Pungent

**Nature**: Justice, forcefulness, unyieldingness, rigidity, stiffness, movement upward, virtue, duty, perseverance, power, charity, dignity, inspiration, virility, authority, ingenuity, abundance, prosperity, originality, vitality, health, protection, control, domination, the spoken word, performing rituals in honor of the seasons, truth seeking, the supernatural, the higher self, following the will of heaven, and acting in accord with the wishes of the people

**Animal symbols**: Horses, dragons, lions, elephants, bears, and cranes

**Plants**: Chrysanthemums, pears, pines, lotuses, orchids, and the fruit of trees

**Color**: White and bright colors

**Season**: Autumn

**Time of day**: Evening

**Direction**: Northwest in the Northern Hemisphere, southwest in the Southern Hemisphere

**Objects**: Watches, stamps, jewels, gold, jade, pearls, ice, and objects made of metal

**Buildings/environments**: Capital buildings, parliaments, temples, geometric designs, fortresses, congress halls, ancestral halls, and altars

The Heaven trigram is also known as "the Creative" and is symbolic of pure yang energy. It consists of three solid yang lines and symbolizes the creative impulse of Heaven where the sky, humanity, and earth are all complete yang. It represents the Taoist concept of the divine, the energy of the cosmos that brings a myriad of things into being. It is very active and initiating.

Heaven represents guidance and the liberating hand of truth. It helps us discriminate between truth and falsehood, allowing us to perceive reality. The full force of Heaven's energy can express itself as a strong moral, religious, or intuitive nature. However, the lack of any yielding energy can result in a one-sided quality, sternness, lack of earthly sensibilities or imagination, or a social and emotional naïveté.

In the context of politics, **Qian** stands for peace. In the realm of agriculture, it signifies success with the necessary tasks and predicts an abundant harvest. Weather (the sky) is clear and normal, and humanity works with all its strength. The fields—representing the earth—are well tilled and well watered. The trigram also symbolizes good fortune.

In terms of health the Heaven trigram relates to the lungs. We absorb Heaven through our breath—we literally take Heaven in through our lungs, inhaling not only oxygen, but also all the radiations of Heaven, the fine vibrations of the cosmos. The lungs, corresponding to the Chinese element of Metal, are home to the iron in our red blood. Iron attracts oxygen: yin attracts yang. Heaven is truly inside us!

To align ourselves with the energy of the Heaven trigram, we must speak and seek the truth. Physically, we need to practice deep breathing and meditation. We may also sing, chant, play music, and say our prayers to tap into the harmonic, vibrational world of Heaven. Our diet must provide a healthy quantity of good-quality iron.

In intellectual terms, we can sharpen our "metal" through precision work, accurate calculations, and a clean and orderly working environment. Artistically, this trigram is associated with geometric patterns and classically proportioned artwork.

In terms of feng shui, it is associated with the helpful people in our life, altruistic viewpoints, and the consideration of the well-being of others and our environment. It encourages us to indulge in selfless giving and the creation of a higher awareness inside ourselves; it gives us the sense of being connected with Heaven. The key to Heaven is gratitude for everything, good and bad.

## WORKBOOK EXERCISES

Reflect on the following questions and make notes in your I Ching journal:

1. Write down five things you associate with the word "heaven"—this could include feelings, thoughts, sounds, smells, environments, special places, or objects.
2. Now read "A Key to the Heaven Trigram" again (pages 47–48). Are there any more things you would like to add to this list?
3. Write down three times in your life when you have felt you portrayed good leadership qualities.
4. In what areas of your life are there leadership opportunities? For example, in your family, community, or business. List three.
5. With you as a leader, what benefits do you see for yourself and other people? Write down three for each.
6. How do you help other people? Write down three ways you have helped people in the past week.
7. How do you access the divine? For example, through music, singing, dancing, chanting, meditation, prayer, art, or photography? Name three.
8. Are you currently using any of the above to access the divine? Why or why not?
9. Qian symbolizes honesty, truth, success, and good fortune. How can you relate your present situation in life to this trigram?

# EARTH (KUN)
## A KEY TO THE EARTH TRIGRAM

**People**: Women aged forty-six or older, wives, mothers, wise women, farmers, servants, midwives, butlers, doctors and herbalists, nurses, nannies, kindergarten teachers, social workers, housekeepers, potters, real estate brokers, and craftspeople

**Health**: Abdomen, digestive system, spleen, stomach, and shoulders

**Element**: Earth

**Sense**: Taste

**Flavor**: Sweet

**Nature**: Elegance, passivity, surrender, devotion, service, hollowness, downward motion, dependability, support, calmness, responsiveness, fertility, quietness, docility, nurture, thriftiness, acceptance, maturity, mildness, security, softness, adaptability, yieldingness, flexibility, openness, vulnerability, delicacy, loyalty, humility, mothering, kindness

**Animal symbols**: Cows, oxen, sheep, and ants

**Plants**: Squash, sweet potatoes, cotton, straw, and grass

**Color**: Yellow and the rich colors of the earth

**Season**: Late summer (the period of ripening)

**Time of day**: Afternoon

**Direction**: Southwest in the Northern Hemisphere, northwest in the Southern Hemisphere

**Objects**: Cloth, silk, cauldrons, wagons, houses, homes, handles, crowds, broken things, agricultural equipment, clay, digging tools, land, and domestic appliances

**Buildings/environments**: Religious communities, clubs, associations, societies, villages, small towns, consulting rooms, ghettos, sheds, kitchens, domestic dwellings, and rural environments

Also known as "the Receptive," this trigram symbolizes pure yin energy—the female force. The Earth trigram consists of three broken lines, rendering this the most yin of the eight trigrams. Traditionally, it is represented by the docility and strength of a mare or mother cow.

*Kun* represents the responsive energy of the universe. It is through this responsive energy that the creative energy (the Heaven trigram) manifests and is able to be creative. Earth completely absorbs the celestial energy and materializes it into forms, shapes, textures, and tastes. In creation, the function of Heaven and Earth are equally essential, neither being greater than the other. They complement each other and work together to bring into being all that is.

Although Kun indicates a character or condition that is totally yielding, nurturing, and receptive, this does not mean that this is the weakest possible trigram. In the *Tao Te Ching*, the great sage Lao Tsu extols the virtues and unconquerable strength of the yielding feminine principle. The Earth trigram represents unconditional acceptance, as exemplified by the life and teachings of Christ, and the force of passive resistance, such as the approach Gandhi employed in achieving independence for India.

This trigram suggests getting in touch with our feelings rather than our rational thoughts. It is also the power of the mundane: food, clothing, and domestic bliss. It is the practical world and the growing and gathering of food. It is the image of a pot of soup on the stove and a warm and cozy home. It means fortifying the center, stabilizing, grounding, and anchoring ourselves in the reality of the world.

## WORKBOOK EXERCISES

Reflect on the following questions and make notes in your I Ching journal:

1. Write down five things you associate with the word "earth"—this could include feelings, thoughts, sounds, smells, environments, special places, or objects.
2. Now read "A Key to the Earth Trigram" again (pages 51–52). Are there any more things you would like to add to this list?
3. Name five ways you show respect to the planet Earth. For example, do you recycle, are you aware of environmental issues, do you waste resources?
4. Describe three times in your life when you felt supported and nurtured. Who do you support and nurture? Name three people. From what areas of your life do they come? For example, your family, childhood friends, and coworkers.
5. Do you allow yourself to be open, vulnerable, and intimate with others? How often?
6. Kun is the key to empathy, compassion, and understanding. How can you relate your present situation in life to this trigram?

# THUNDER (ZHEN)
## A KEY TO THE THUNDER TRIGRAM

**People:** Eldest sons, males aged between thirty-one and forty-five, prime movers, action men, those with "act now, think later" attitudes, motivated people, performers, street actors, the idealistic, the expansive, the thoughtless, the tactless, the enthusiastic, the aggressive, the angry, coaches, mentors, our first teachers, our parental influence, engineers, architects, carpenters, sales and advertising people

**Health:** Feet, liver, and gallbladder

**Element:** Wood

**Sense:** Sight

**Flavor:** Sour

**Nature:** Agitation, awakenings, exaltations, elevation, excitement, impetus, stimulation, vehemence, impulses, thrusts, volition, beginnings of movement, thunder and lightning, electricity, vigor, confrontation, renewal, explosions, surprises, shocks, liberation, noisiness, new projects, imminent revolutions, initiating momentum, and earthquakes

**Animal symbols:** Dragons (in the East), eagles, ponies, snakes, and mosquitoes

**Plants:** Young bamboo, sprouts, and reeds

**Color:** Bright green and turquoise

**Season:** Spring

**Time of day:** Early morning

**Direction:** East for both hemispheres (the rising sun)

**Objects:** Plows, trumpets, pistols, gunpowder, and firecrackers

**Buildings/environments:** Pagodas, skyscrapers, lecture halls, workshops, and forests

As it implies rapidity, speed, and quick movement, **Zhen**, also known as "the Arousing" or "the Awakening," corresponds to sudden diseases, pain in the nerves, illnesses of the sensory system, the motor system, the sympathetic nervous system, the lower extremities, the tendons, the gallbladder, and liver yang. It is also associated with birth, growth, and development.

Where psychological reactions are concerned, sudden fits of anger and rage may be indicated by this trigram. This trigram depicts the energy of early spring, bursting forth with fresh vitality and new growth. The yang line at the bottom illustrates a primal, irrepressible strength. The two yielding lines above offer no resistance to this strongly rooted impulse, which results in a constant energetic growth in a straight upward direction. This produces a strong sense of linking directly with the cosmos and with nature.

The key to this trigram is action—or, more specifically, action with understanding and compassion with self-knowledge. The need to stop sitting around talking and to take action is its strong message. However, it also shows the need to be aware of our motivations, our urges, our cravings, and our intentions. The strength indicated by the yang line can get out of control—like a teenage son unaware of his limitations. When correctly initiated and channeled, this energy is unstoppable.

The thunder in our lives is related to our teachers, who influence and guide us. The trigram advises us to choose our teachers wisely. We need to avoid negative company and those who will not help us channel our cravings, desires, and impulsive nature.

Zhen tells us we should join a group rather than trying to do it alone. Social interaction is important. Your rage at injustice in the world can be directed into positive outcomes. Take care of your liver and avoid too many stimulants, since they make you angry. Move your body and learn to dance. Thunder is a wake-up call, reminding you that you are an energetic manifestation of life—you are the spark.

## ☯ WORKBOOK EXERCISES

Reflect on the following questions and make notes in your I Ching journal:

1. Write down five things you associate with the word "thunder"—this could include feelings, thoughts, sounds, smells, environments, special places, or objects.
2. Now read "A Key to the Thunder Trigram" again (pages 55–56). Are there any more things you would like to add to this list?
3. On what occasions are you spontaneous?
4. In what areas of your life do you initiate new things? Now name three new things you have recently initiated and three new things you would like to initiate.
5. In what types of situations do you hold back, even when you strongly desire to start something?
6. How do you feel when you see injustice around you? What do you do as a result?
7. How often do you feel that your life is unraveling without you thinking about it?
8. Zhen is a trigger for things to grow and for taking action. How can you relate your present situation in life to this trigram?

# WIND (XUN)
## A KEY TO THE WIND TRIGRAM

**People**: Eldest daughters, women aged thirty to forty-five, those with broad foreheads, those with breezy characters, business executives, salespeople, the upwardly mobile, planners, dance instructors, motivational speakers, poets, artists, and bohemians; also people involved in distribution companies, advertising agencies, construction businesses, and personal growth seminars

**Health**: Liver and gallbladder, the thighs, hips, and waist area, strong odors, muscles, tendons, and excess movement in the body, such as trembling or shaking

**Element**: Wood

**Sense**: Sight

**Flavor**: Sour

**Nature**: Romance, dispersion, vehemence, pursuit of gain, decisions, lying, profound influences and effects, obedience, pervasiveness, gaseousness, growth, maturation, an enlivening, upward movement, very light forces, transformation, bending, politeness, courtesy, tidiness, changeability, progress, interaction, gentleness, pervasion, ease, keen-sightedness, formality, fleetingness, and affection

**Animal symbols**: Hairless animals, chickens, worms, daddy longlegs, and flies

**Plants**: Bamboo, blossoming plants, and green, unripe fruits

**Color**: Dark green

**Season**: Late spring

**Time of day**: Midmorning

**Direction**: Southeast in the Northern Hemisphere (the position of the morning sun), northeast in the Southern Hemisphere

**Objects**: Long rectangular shapes, Jupiter, vacuum cleaners, fans, bellows, rope, showcases, air conditioners, wooden toys, and wind instruments

**Buildings/environments**: Woods, vegetation, markets, art galleries, sacred places for rituals, hallways, nurseries, personal growth centers, rumpus rooms, and family rooms

To understand the energy of the **Xun** trigram, imagine the wind blowing over the ground and the roots penetrating the earth. This trigram is also known as "the Gentle" and its energy acts mildly, penetrating everywhere like a fresh warm breeze in the morning—the best of weather. This trigram represents discipline and dedication to the way of nature and raises the question: Do you honor nature?

The two yang lines above the broken yin line show a reservoir of energy from above, indicating a strong cosmological and mental force moving on a soft yin base. The activity of the two yang lines above is constant and consistent. The yielding line at the base signifies a withdrawing of energy and possibly a weakness at the root, producing the tendency to need continuous replenishing of physical or material vitality and support.

Psychologically, Xun is associated with despondency, impatience, lack of motivation, and anger. When in harmony, it generates humor and our ability to laugh at the human predicament and the paradoxes of life.

Xun corresponds to the element of Wood and also suggests the liver, the thighs, and the parasympathetic nervous system. The energy of the liver is considered the "general of the army" in Chinese medicine. It is the great strategist.

Spiritually, the liver is connected with vision—with seeing the bigger view. Once we have locked into a vision, we can then proceed to make the decisions that will transform our vision into reality. We must remember that one grain of rice produces a thousand grains of rice. Abundance is a natural phenomenon and should not be denied. Start an enterprise. Share something useful with others. It does not matter how big or small it is, since there are no winners or losers. There is only experience.

Feng shui advice: Sit facing the morning sun. Plant a tree there and watch it grow.

*Rouse the awareness within, and the tiger roars wind.*
*Wash away the dust from the senses,*
*And the dragon makes rain.*
Li Daoqun

## WORKBOOK EXERCISES

Reflect on the following questions and make notes in your I Ching journal:

1. Write down five things you associate with the word "wind"—this could include feelings, thoughts, sounds, smells, environments, special places, or objects.
2. Now read "A Key to the Wind Trigram" again (pages 59–60). Are there any more things you would like to add to this list?
3. Do you feel you are rewarded for your endeavors in life? How? Do you feel you have blessings coming your way?
4. What is your financial situation—do you have money in the bank? A cash flow? An enterprise?
5. Do you think you are mentally stimulating to those around you? In what circumstances? If you do not feel mentally stimulated, how could this change?
6. Xun is considered to be the wealth and prosperity trigram. How can you relate your present situation in life to this trigram?

## WATER (KAN)
### A KEY TO THE WATER TRIGRAM

**People**: Middle sons, men aged sixteen to thirty, diplomats, writers, playwrights, sailors, plumbers, fishermen, autoworkers, drivers, criminals, spies, music and radio personalities, newspeople, and those in the travel, printing, and oil industries

**Health**: Ears, kidneys, bladder, reproductive organs, spine, bone marrow, and hair on the head

**Element**: Water

**Sense**: Hearing

**Flavor**: Salty

**Nature**: Great forward movement like a river, vitality, journeys, careers, libido, adventures, concealment, translucence, adaptability, fluidity, stretching and flowing, courage, cleverness, stumbling, prone to accidents, danger, difficulty, darkness, coldness, cruelty, hard work, secrets, sleep, rest, dormancy, embryos, death, uncertainty, anxiety, fear, instinct, deception, clouds, obscurity, dreaminess, hindrance, confusion, dilemmas, disasters, crises, perils, obstacles, troubles, afflictions, meanness, isolation, phobias, calamities, treason, poverty, risks, adversities, antisocial attitudes, cryptic meanings, and enemies

**Animal symbols**: Dolphins, whales, bats, and pigs

**Plants**: Water plants, trees that are solid and firm at the core, seaweed, and seeds

**Color**: Black

**Season**: Winter

**Time of day**: Night

**Direction**: Toward the cold regions—north in the Northern Hemisphere and south in the Southern Hemisphere

**Objects**: Bows, wheels, moon, camouflage, puzzles, swimwear, shoes, underwear, bicycles, boats, drums, ink, coal, poisons, belts, tapes, CD-ROMs, and refrigerators

**Buildings/environments**: Dams, ditches, canals, oceans, rivers, trenches, abysses, flooding, pits, holes, depression, recesses, storage tanks, canyons, shafts, waterfalls, breweries, hotels and inns, rehabilitation centers, greenhouses, bathhouses, laundries, bathrooms and toilets, bedrooms, rehearsal rooms, burial chambers, and travel agencies

Also known as "the Depth," "the Dangerous," or "the Abysmal," this trigram indicates a primal state that precedes all growth. It also symbolizes times of our life when we feel that we are entering into the unknown. The trigram represents the risk of life—but without water we would perish.

The trigram for water is composed of a central yang line enclosed by two yin lines. This wonderfully unadorned symbol reveals the inherent nature of water, which on the surface is soft and yielding (yin qualities), but which has the power to dissolve even the hardest rock (a yang characteristic). Yang is at the central position, indicating movement. Water never stops—the ocean never stops pulsating and the river moves forward while maintaining its yielding nature.

This trigram shows a deeply hidden reserve of strength within the external appearance of passivity, fluidity, and constant flux. It illustrates hidden vitality stored in primal dormancy, obscured by the passive cold above and below. The opposite of the Fire trigram, which shows all energy revealed in maturity and on the surface, the Water trigram shows energy in its origins.

If such a trigram were associated with a particular type of person, it would describe one who is well-developed: socially and outwardly gentle (as he or she is surrounded and sheathed by soft yin elements) but extremely strong at the core. Water is humility itself— it listens to everyone, it penetrates everything, and it crosses all obstacles.

*Kan* also corresponds to the diseases of the kidneys, bladder, bones, and body fluids, such as edema. It also suggests the lower abdomen, the marrow, the nose, ears, gums, and hair. Psychologically, it indicates anxiety, fear, and tension.

In Chinese medicine, the emotion of fear is housed in the kidney qi. To restore the kidney qi and revive your desire and drive, avoid cold foods, refrigerated drinks, excess fruits (cooling), excess raw foods, excess liquids, and sugar. Incorporate into your diet warm drinks, slightly cooked foods, warming soups, seafood, and warming herbs such as ginger.

# WORKBOOK EXERCISES

Reflect on the following questions and make notes in your I Ching journal:

1. Write down five things you associate with the word "water"—this could include feelings, thoughts, sounds, smells, environments, special places, or objects.
2. Now read "A Key to the Water Trigram" again (pages 63–64). Are there any more things you would like to add to this list?
3. What is your journey?
4. Do you ever feel you are struggling against the tide? Describe three situations in which you have felt this way.
5. Do you believe you have found your true pathway in life yet? If so, write down what this pathway is; if not, name five things that you believe are keeping you from finding it.
6. What does danger mean to you—for example, numbing fear or new opportunities? How comfortable are you in these situations?
7. Kan represents the dangerous and venturing into the unknown. How can you relate your present situation in life to this trigram?

## FIRE (LI)
### A KEY TO THE FIRE TRIGRAM

**People**: Middle daughters, women aged sixteen to thirty, movie stars, clairvoyants, intellectuals, fundamentalists, pharmacists, editors, chefs, fashion designers, the nobility, opticians, hairdressers, war correspondents, comedians, celebrities; also people in the entertainment and beauty industries, movies and television, the media, public relations, politics, religion, and the emergency services

**Health**: Eyes, heart, tongue, small intestines, consciousness, and the circulatory system

**Element**: Fire

**Sense**: Smell

**Flavor**: Bitter

**Nature**: Radiation, warmth, recognition, passion, talent, clarity, expansion, apexes, peaks, extremes, awareness, fame, uniqueness, luminescence, enlightenment, nirvana, discrimination, intelligence, togetherness, patriotism, dependency, attachment, superficial thought, lack of substance, hollowness at the center, incandescence, reason, insight, prudence, dynamism, charisma, inflammations and fever, hysteria, hyperactivity, loss of control, volatility, magnetism, passion, bliss, ecstasy, alchemy, mythologies, legends, storytelling, public speaking, celebrations, utopia, immortals, and deities

**Animal symbols**: Flying birds, animals with hard shells, turtles, crabs, snails, oysters, goldfish, crickets, butterflies, cats, foxes, gray herons, peacocks, and magpies

**Plants**: Maple trees, cherries, roses, and trees that are hollow

**Color**: Red and purple

**Season**: Midsummer

**Time of day**: Noon

**Direction**: Toward the warm regions—south in the Northern Hemisphere and north in the Southern Hemisphere

**Objects**: The sun, logos, decorations, stocks and shares, paintings, movies, calligraphy, ovens, leather, neon lights, parades, and parties

**Buildings/environments**: The Olympic Games, Hollywood, stadiums, stock markets, deserts, theaters, beauty salons, church towers, universities, power stations, nuclear and atomic facilities, chemical factories, bushfires, and wars

Also known as "the Clinging," this trigram is the symbol of light and heat. Its attribute is brightness. *Li* represents intelligence and illumination and is called our consciousness. The trigram for fire consists of two yang lines surrounding a central yin line. This implies that fire, which is very yang on the surface—hot and active—is actually unstable and easily extinguished. The yang nature of fire needs fuel to work; it needs to attach to something of the material world that is yin.

This can create overattachment and addictions or clinging. The middle yin line can manifest as a need for social, emotional, or environmental support, collaboration, or confirmation.

Li corresponds with circulatory diseases and cardiovascular conditions, as well as the diseases of the small intestine, tongue, and eyes. It suggests inflammation, fever, and problems with the metabolism. Extreme forms of delirium and hysteria can be indicated by this trigram. All mental diseases are related to this trigram.

Fire is our awareness and clarity of insight. Fire is a modification of the Heaven trigram, indicating that our awareness and consciousness has its roots in the celestial but the celestial is now attached to Earth (the middle line). It is easy to get trapped here. Like fire, we need to "attach" to things in order to fuel ourselves. Clarity of vision comes from the heart and is not filled with the things of the mind. We are subjected to earthly influences, but these are not our true nature. We become conditioned by society and begin to identify ourselves with its imposed labels. Fire relates to the liberation of the self. This is expressed in the Taoist saying "Being beyond the world while living in the world."

## WORKBOOK EXERCISES

Reflect on the following questions and make notes in your I Ching journal:

1. Write down five things you associate with the word "fire"—this could include feelings, thoughts, sounds, smells, environments, special places, or objects.
2. Now read "A Key to the Fire Trigram" again (pages 67–68). Are there any more things you would like to add to this list?
3. What do the following mean to you—talent, self-worth, and fame?
4. On a scale of one to ten, how important do you rate passion in your life?
5. What makes you feel passionate? Name ten things.
6. What is your definition of bliss?
7. Write down five ways you can create more bliss in your life.
8. Li represents intelligence and illumination. How can you relate your present situation in life to this trigram?

## MOUNTAIN (GEN)
### A KEY TO THE MOUNTAIN TRIGRAM

**People**: Youngest sons, boys up to fifteen years old, children, security guards, wise teachers, spiritual guides, bachelors, mountaineers, prisoners, laboratory workers, inventors, revolutionaries, and clerical workers

**Health**: Fingers, hands, stomach, and spleen

**Element**: Earth

**Sense**: Taste

**Flavor**: Sweet

**Nature**: Accomplishment, rest, halting, meditation, stillness, inner reserve, inertia, faithfulness, downward motion, retreat, stubbornness, obstacles, heaviness, concentration, silence, contemplation, deep thinking, research, science, property development and investment, social infrastructure, long-term investment and development, slow accumulation of wealth, simplicity, thriftiness, dignity, prudence, stagnation, pressure, conservatism, inner knowledge, accumulated wisdom, and philosophies of the world

**Animal symbols**: Dogs, birds with strong bills

**Plants**: Trees with many joints, oak and walnut trees

**Color**: White soil

**Season**: Late winter and early spring

**Time of day**: Early morning

**Direction**: Northeast in the Northern Hemisphere, southeast in the Southern Hemisphere

**Objects**: Gold found in mines, canned foods, stones, tables, umbrellas, safes, strong rooms, cupboards, jewelry boxes, treasure chests, filing cabinets, records departments, old wine, and preserved foods

**Buildings/environments**: Gates and doors, warehouses, cemeteries, mountainous areas, mortuaries, department stores, meditation centers, spiritual retreat centers, ashrams, and banks

The shape of this trigram depicts the outline of a mountain surmounted by the sky with a yang line at the top supported by two yin lines underneath. The lower two lines look like an entrance into a cave in the mountain. Yin lines are slow moving; it takes thousands of years to accumulate the earth qi to make a mountain.

This trigram, also known as "the Stable," shows a quiet depth of passivity, receptivity, and accumulation without movement and contemplation, encased within a solid, unyielding, stable surface strength, as exemplified by the mighty mountain. The yang line at the top denotes a direction of mental agility, yet it rests on a base of slow, heavy, or more stationary physical and social forces. In terms of the years and seasons, this depicts the time immediately before spring when the softening of the hard winter soil is hidden under the residual veneer of winter's hardened brilliance. The ice is cracking, but fresh movement is not yet apparent. Symbolizing hidden strength and concealed intelligence, this trigram is also called "the Revolutionary."

If we focus on our inner nature, our true self, and our substance, our character will slowly deepen, like the minds of the old wise ones who have already been through the various cycles of life. They have scars but their smile is clear. *Gen* asks: Is your mind clear of clutter or do you feel stagnant or congested? Is your life just a series of fickle moment-to-moment graspings at the material world?

Going to the mountain implies taking the time to learn to develop yourself and honors your capacity to regenerate. After taking this time, you can return to the commercial world feeling like a new person—refreshed, changed, and revolutionized. You have a choice before you. One pathway leads to the mountain, to sacredness, to oneness, while another leads to endless fragmentation. You must choose which way to go.

## WORKBOOK EXERCISES

Reflect on the following questions and make notes in your I Ching journal:

1. Write down five things you associate with the word "mountain"—this could include feelings, thoughts, sounds, smells, environments, special places, or objects.
2. Now read "A Key to the Mountain Trigram" again (pages 71–72). Are there any more things you would like to add to this list?
3. Where do you go to obtain knowledge? Name three sources.
4. Answer the following questions: Who am I? Where do I come from?
5. Do you take time in your life to spiritually evolve? If so, how? If not, why not?
6. Is there a place you go when you want to retreat from the world? Describe this place and what it means to you.
7. What does sacredness mean to you?
8. Ken represents stability and strength. How can you relate your present situation in life to this trigram?

## LAKE (DUI)
### A KEY TO THE LAKE TRIGRAM

**People**: Youngest daughters, girls up to fifteen years old, female shamans, magicians, sorceresses, concubines, fortune-tellers, psychics, singers, cabaret performers, store clerks, lawyers, legal workers, astrologers, dentists, people involved in the restaurant, leisure, and resort businesses, and people engaged in esoteric studies; also, the influence of women

**Health**: Mouth, teeth, lungs, large intestine, and skin

**Element**: Metal

**Sense**: Touch

**Flavor**: Spicy

**Nature**: Gracefulness, serenity, tranquillity, sensuality, talkativeness, narcissism, and gaiety

**Animal symbols**: Monkeys, deer, sheep, elks, mice, and horned animals

**Plants**: Magnolias, gardenias, ponds with plants, mangroves, weeds, and fruit drooping from trees

**Color**: Red

**Season**: Fall (harvest time)

**Time of day**: Evening

**Direction**: West for both hemispheres (sunset)

**Objects**: Calibration devices, swords, erotic and sensual items, bells, brass instruments, scrap metal, yin or flexible metal (such as copper), antiques, and luxury items

**Buildings/environments**: Courthouses, unsafe and run-down buildings, hard and salty soils, bars, pubs, cafés, brothels, gambling halls, casinos, racetracks, amusement parks, and houses crammed with many luxurious items

In Chinese, **Dui** means a variety of things, such as a reservoir of water, marshlands, swamps, rice fields, radiating cheerfulness, and speaking with joy. It has connotations of pleasure and the good things in life; it embodies delight. The Lake is the symbol of gravity and the absorption of heavenly cosmological qi.

To the ancient Chinese, a marsh exemplified a place of joyous life with water, plants, fish, birds, and other animals. Today it also connotes pleasure, a time of enjoyment, entertainment, and fun. It relates to going on vacation and enjoying the fruits of your endeavors.

The trigram, with its two solid yang lines at the bottom and one broken yin line at the top, symbolizes a rooted, stabilized base of strength with a fluid, yielding surface, represented as the reflective surface of the Lake. The yielding line on top can indicate a special receptivity to spiritual or even psychic influences and a strong capacity for reflection and serenity.

This trigram is associated with psychic abilities and intuitive sciences such as feng shui and astrology. The full yang of the two lower lines, the physical and practical conditions, can manifest as emphatic passions and powerful physical, sensory, emotional, or social appetites. These lines are always seeking to balance the contemplative, reflecting surface of the soft line on top. The trigram corresponds to the realm of health and medicine and to diseases of the mouth, the oral cavity, the digestive system, and the reproductive system.

The Lake's creativity can enrich all aspects of daily life and activities. Whatever one's occupation, creativity is the breath of moment-to-moment reality and the enjoyment of the present. Make everything you do creative and inspiring. Discover the pattern of the whole universe in the palm of your hand. Learn to breathe deeply, relax, and reflect upon yourself. The Lake is an inspiring place to visit in the mind's eye. It is formed high up in the mountains, close to the clouds. On the surface we see the reflection of the moon and stars within us. This is our playground, where our children are allowed to play and have fun. These children symbolize our current projects and creative endeavors, which can take a quantum leap in these surroundings. It is an atmosphere free from stress, in which we may engage with the creative process of life again. Keep the image of this trigram close to you.

## WORKBOOK EXERCISES

Reflect on the following questions and make notes in your I Ching journal:

1. Write down five things you associate with the word "lake"—this could include feelings, thoughts, sounds, smells, environments, special places, or objects.
2. Now read "A Key to the Lake Trigram" again (pages 75–76). Are there any more things you would like to add to this list?
3. Are you connected with your inner intuitive feelings? How could you become more so?
4. Write down five ways you enjoy yourself. Could you enjoy yourself more? Write down three ways you could do this.
5. Could you make every process in life an enjoyable one? Name five things you would have to do to achieve this.
6. Are you drawn to the mysterious? What do you consider the secrets of life?
7. What is your "magic potion"?
8. What is your greatest pleasure in life?
9. Dui represents joy and serenity. How can you relate your present situation in life to this trigram?

## TRIGRAMS AND SOCIAL INTERACTIONS

The trigrams have other associations that help us understand how qi flows around us. We can connect with nature's powerful harmony and balance if we choose to observe these manifestations.

Where our social interactions are concerned, the trigrams correspond with certain family dynamics. The father is symbolized by the Heaven trigram. This trigram consists of three unbroken yang lines and represents the most yang energy among the eight trigrams. The mother is symbolized by the Earth trigram, which is a stack of three broken yin lines, indicating the most yin energy among the trigrams.

From these "parents," three yang and three yin family members are generated. The yin or yang line that is in the minority for each trigram is said to rule it. For instance, the Water trigram has one yang line in it. Therefore, it is one of the yang family members.

The reason for this is the Taoist concept of the small controlling the large, the hidden controlling the obvious, the dot in the yin symbol controlling the yang and vice versa.

Each of the three yang family members, or brothers, is believed to correspond with the energy of a particular type of male child born into a family—the eldest, middle, and youngest sons. The position of the unbroken yang line will determine the order of the male children. The trigram that has an unbroken line in the first (bottom) position represents the eldest son and is symbolic of Thunder. The trigram that has the unbroken yang or male line in the middle position corresponds with the middle son and indicates Water. A male line at the top position refers to the youngest son and the trigram of the Mountain.

Similarly, a broken line as the first (bottom) line represents the second-most yin

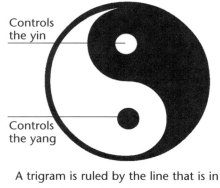

Controls
the yin

Controls
the yang

A trigram is ruled by the line that is in the minority, based on the Taoist concept of the small controlling the large, as in yin and yang.

family member or sister—the eldest daughter. The trigram that corresponds with the eldest daughter is that of Wind. The trigram representing the middle daughter and Fire has a broken line in the middle position, while the trigram symbolizing the youngest daughter and the Lake has a broken line in the top position.

The trigrams are arranged in pairs, in order of opposites—Heaven with Earth, Thunder with Wind, Water with Fire, and Mountain with Lake. As illustrated below, if a line of one pair of trigrams is yang, the corresponding line of the trigram's opposite in the same position will be yin. The correspondences between family members and trigrams are set out below.

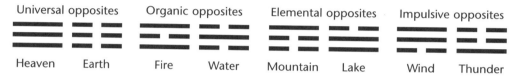

| Universal opposites | | Organic opposites | | Elemental opposites | | Impulsive opposites | |
|---|---|---|---|---|---|---|---|
| Heaven | Earth | Fire | Water | Mountain | Lake | Wind | Thunder |

The masculine (initiating, yang) polarizes with the feminine (responsive, yin).

Father (Heaven)                    Mother (Earth)
Eldest son (Thunder)               Eldest daughter (Wind)
Middle son (Water)                 Middle daughter (Fire)
Youngest son (Mountain)            Youngest daughter (Lake)

## WORKBOOK EXERCISES

1. Which trigram do you think is most like yourself? Why do you identify with it? Think about:
   • your spiritual nature
   • your emotions and psychology
   • your health and the world of your senses—the world of material things
2. How do you manifest your energy in the world? Describe which trigram best fits this process.

## CHAPTER FOUR

# HOW TO CONSTRUCT A HEXAGRAM

*Develop the skills for constructing hexagrams. Learn the methods of casting.*
*How to identify your hexagram.*

In the last chapter, we examined the eight trigrams. These can be combined in various configurations to form up to sixty-four hexagrams. Each hexagram, the powerful and resonant unit of meaning in the I Ching, is composed of two of these eight trigrams—a lower trigram and an upper trigram. The lower trigram indicates the inside or back of the situation or the circumstances prior to the situation. The upper trigram signifies the outside or front of the situation or future circumstances regarding the situation. Knowing about this composition can help us make an intuitive interpretation of the hexagrams and enable us to interpret the energy pattern that surrounds the situation in which we are involved.

It is the hexagrams that carry the wisdom of the I Ching. When you consult the I Ching, you are trying to discover which hexagram is relevant to your search for enlightenment about your life.

## METHODS OF CASTING

To determine the relevant hexagram, you will need to perform a casting. This is done by throwing coins or using similar means while thinking of your question. For each throw of the coin, you get a result that can be depicted by either a yin or yang line. Throwing the coins six times will give you six lines, which together will form a hexagram.

Before we examine this process, let us look briefly at the methods commonly used for casting hexagrams; coin casting is only one of them. Traditionally, a bunch of yarrow sticks were used. This is a very time-consuming method and for this reason the bead-casting method is given here (see pages 86–87), as it comes closest to the results obtained using yarrow sticks. Today there are even computer programs for casting the I Ching. According to Taoist masters, coins are a noble way to consult the I Ching. They have a good, balanced energy and can be charged with your vibrations.

## THE COINS

When you consult the oracle, a certain energy flows through you. This energy will be communicated to the coins you use. When you become proficient at consulting the I Ching, you will realize that at the moment of throwing the coins some kind of intense connection takes place. During this highly connected state, a certain vibration is imprinted into the coins. Each time you use the coins with this connection, more energy will reach them. The more your coins are charged, the easier it will be to reach a pure connection with the true source of the I Ching and the more meaningful the answers will be.

## SELECTING COINS

If you change coins all the time, the refinement of the coin energy can never take place. If you use coins from money currently in circulation, they will be full of vibrations of all kinds. Money changes hands all the time—in astrological terms, money is a mercurial, or changeable, principle. The act of changing hands is likely to produce vibrations that interfere with your attempts to connect with the oracle.

Your choice of coins for use in reading the I Ching is therefore of great importance. You should use three identical coins. Anything containing iron is to be avoided, since in most cases iron (the metal of Mars) is not favorable to higher connections. Subtle beings such as the fairies are said to hate iron and to avoid it at any cost. Copper, in contrast, being the metal of Venus, is excellent for receiving and storing subtle vibrations. In India, the pots and various tools and vessels used for *pujas* and *yajnas* (rituals of connection to the worlds of the gods) are usually made of copper and never iron or any alloy containing iron. Gold, the first choice, is often far too expensive for the user, but copper is an effective substitute.

If you do need to use coins that were in circulation, it is a good idea to let them soak for a few days in salted water to purify them. Some people like to use old Chinese coins, which can be purchased from some coin shops. Even though most of these coins are not ancient, they have the advantage of never having been used as currency. The shape of the coins—a square within a circle—is also relevant. The circle stands for the sky and Heaven, and the square for the Earth. There is no need to try to clean Chinese coins with chemicals. Just use them in a regular fashion—the sweat from your hands will soon restore their shine.

## USING THE LEFT HAND

Some people always throw the coins with their left hand, as the left side of the body corresponds to the right hemisphere of the brain, which is said to be more intuitive and inspirational than the left hemisphere of the brain.

In the Tantric traditions of India, the left side of the body is ruled by the *nadi*, or energy channel, called *ida*. The ida nadi directs the consciousness toward inner worlds. Other channels externalize consciousness, directing it toward the material world. The purpose of the I Ching is to fathom the knowledge of spiritual worlds. Using the left hand, on the side of the ida nadi, will facilitate this. The left hand is also said to be "the hand of the heart," and it is precisely when your questions come from the heart, not from the head, that the I Ching oracle will give spectacular answers.

## RITUAL INSTRUMENTS

Treat your coins with respect, like ritual instruments—which they indeed are. This will help to refine their energy. Take some time to ensure that your coins receive positive attention and focused energy from yourself. The more they can be linked with your higher self, the better results you will get.

Be wary also of sharing your coins. This can cause a confusion of energies and will reduce the purity of communication with the oracle. If another person handles them with disrespect or uses them to ask questions based on greed, your hard work may be lost.

Between I Ching sessions, keep your coins in a container—no metals. A small wooden box is ideal. This will protect them from being contaminated by the energy of other objects. Make sure that you keep the box in a quiet place.

# COIN-CASTING METHOD

## ASSIGNING VALUES

Assign the value 2 to one side of the coin. This is the yin side, as even numbers are associated with yin. Traditionally, the tail side of a coin is yin.

Assign the value 3 to the other side of the coin. This is the yang side, as odd numbers are associated with yang. Traditionally, the head side of a coin is yang.

Take the three coins in your left hand. Spend a moment to formulate your question. It should be a question that comes from your heart (see page 38). While thinking of your question, throw the three coins.

Add the values assigned to the sides showing and note down the result. It will be either 6, 7, 8, or 9. This will become the first (bottom) line of the hexagram. Some results will give you a changing line—a line where yin or yang can change to its opposite (see pages 90–97).

| Throw | Coin values | Throw value | Line | Changing |
|---|---|---|---|---|
| Tail, Tail, Tail | 2 + 2 + 2 | 6 | —X— | Yes, symbol X |
| Tail, Tail, Head | 2 + 2 + 3 | 7 | ——— | No |
| Tail, Head, Head | 2 + 3 + 3 | 8 | — — | No |
| Head, Head, Head | 3 + 3 + 3 | 9 | —O— | Yes, symbol O |

Gather up the coins and throw them again. Add the values assigned to the sides showing and note down the result, writing it above the result of the first throw.

Repeat the process, writing each result above the previous one, until you have thrown the coins a total of six times.

**Example:**

| | | | |
|---|---|---|---|
| Sixth throw | Tail, Head, Head | 2 + 3 + 3 = 8 | ———  ——— |
| Fifth throw | Tail, Tail, Head | 2 + 2 + 3 = 7 | ————— |
| Fourth throw | Tail, Tail, Tail | 2 + 2 + 2 = 6 | ——✕—— |
| Third throw | Tail, Head, Head | 2 + 3 + 3 = 8 | ———  ——— |
| Second throw | Head, Head, Head | 3 + 3 + 3 = 9 | ——◯—— |
| First throw | Tail, Tail, Head | 2 + 2 + 3 = 7 | ————— |

Draw the hexagram by referring to the table on page 83. The first line of a hexagram is at the bottom, so it is important to remember that a hexagram must always be constructed from the bottom line up. This is believed to symbolize the ascent from earth to heaven, reflecting natural growth. Draw a yin changing line with an "X" in the middle and a yang changing line with an "O" in the middle.

## ASKING YOUR QUESTION

While throwing the coins or beads to construct the hexagram that may answer your question (see pages 37–41), focus on a single question only. If you change your question while throwing the coins, it is better to stop everything and start afresh a minute later. The question should remain exactly the same until you finish constructing the hexagram. Any change of formulation lessens the focus and your connection with the higher beings and may negate the value of the oracle's answer. In particular, it is incorrect to have one main question and then ask a different subquestion each time you throw your coins or beads.

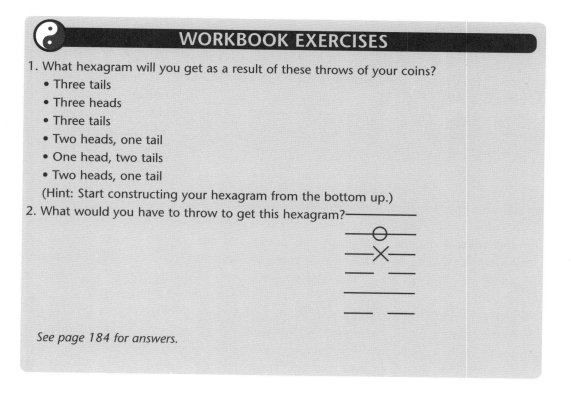

# WORKBOOK EXERCISES

1. What hexagram will you get as a result of these throws of your coins?
   • Three tails
   • Three heads
   • Three tails
   • Two heads, one tail
   • One head, two tails
   • Two heads, one tail
   (Hint: Start constructing your hexagram from the bottom up.)
2. What would you have to throw to get this hexagram?

*See page 184 for answers.*

# BEAD-CASTING METHOD

This is a useful method for casting, as it gets very close to the statistics involved with the older method of casting with yarrow sticks, yet is not nearly as complex.

It is important, however, that the beads you use are all the same size. You could also use identical-shaped crystals, stones, or even buttons.

You will need a bag containing:
- Three red beads
- Seven yellow beads
- Five green beads
- One blue bead

## ASSIGNING A LINE TO EACH BEAD

| Bead | Line | Changing |
|---|---|---|
| Red | ———○——— | Yes, symbol O |
| Yellow | ——— ——— | No |
| Green | ——————— | No |
| Blue | ———X——— | Yes, symbol X |

1. Take the bag of beads in your left hand.
2. Spend a moment formulating your question. It should be a question that comes from your heart.
3. While thinking of your question, take a bead from the bag. Note down the line assigned to this bead, with an "X" in the middle for a yin changing line and an "O" in the middle for a yang changing line. This will become the first line of the hexagram.
4. Return the bead to the bag and pick another bead. Note down the line assigned to this bead, writing it above the result of the first throw.
5. Repeat the process, writing each result above the previous one, until you have done this six times. You have now constructed your hexagram.

## WORKBOOK EXERCISES

1. Look at the hexagram below. It has been constructed by someone using three coins for casting. What throws of the coins produced this hexagram? List them.

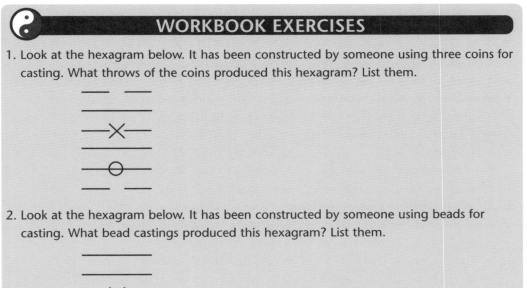

2. Look at the hexagram below. It has been constructed by someone using beads for casting. What bead castings produced this hexagram? List them.

*See page 184 for answers.*

3. Formulate the question you want the I Ching to answer for you, then:
   • Throw three coins six times.
   • Construct your hexagram as you do so.
4. Formulate the question you want the I Ching to answer for you, then:
   • Do a bead casting.
   • Construct your hexagram as you do so.
5. Make notes about each process. Which was more effective for you? Why do you think this was the case?

# IDENTIFYING YOUR HEXAGRAM

There are sixty-four hexagrams, or gua, each assigned with a number ranging from 1 to 64. You will find them in Chapter Six. To identify the number of the hexagram you have constructed through casting, go to the table on page 192. Divide your hexagram into two trigrams. Note the top trigram. Find a match in the upper horizontal row of the table. Now look at the bottom three lines of your hexagram—the lower trigram—and find a match in the vertical row of the table. Trace a line down from the horizontal line and across from the vertical line. Where they meet, you will find a replica of your hexagram and its number.

The table on page 192 also gives the page number in Chapter Six where you will find the description of your hexagram. Read the introduction to Chapter Six and then seek your hexagram. Read its judgment, applying this to the question with which you began your casting. You will be amazed and delighted at the insights that will emerge.

# INTERPRETING THE HEXAGRAMS

When you have constructed your hexagram, take a few minutes just to look at its structure before seeking interpretations. It must be stressed that hexagrams are powerful symbols in themselves and that they work on the psyche when we meditate on them from a spiritual perspective. To derive the greatest benefit from this workbook, it is important to make yourself receptive to the symbols, such as the picture made by the configuration of six broken and/or unbroken lines. Each of the six lines in a hexagram can either be an unbroken yang line or a broken yin line. Taoist symbolism associates the yang line with the phallus and the yin line with the opening of the female sexual organ. The broken yin line has connotations of softness and receptivity, while the straight yang line evokes strength and resistance.

### KEEPING YOUR I CHING TOOLS SAFE

Keep your I Ching journal, this workbook, and your coins or beads wrapped up in a piece of cloth to keep them both safe and private.

# WORKBOOK EXERCISES

1. Now that you have tried both the coin and bead methods, which do you prefer? Why? If one method appeals to you more than the other, work on that method, refining the way you handle the coins or beads.

2. Try the following rituals—or some of your own—before consulting the I Ching:
   • Practice a meditation while holding the coins or beads.
   • Wash the coins or beads under fresh running water and hold them in your hands until they feel warm.
   • Do you feel that you get more accurate readings if you practice these rituals?

3. Do you feel moved to try some other casting method? If so, specify this in your I Ching journal.

## CHAPTER FIVE

# ADVANCED HEXAGRAM READINGS

*Discover the deeper meanings of hexagrams. What are changing lines, progressed hexagrams, and nuclear hexagrams?*

W hen you construct a hexagram that contains changing lines, these lines present you with the possibility of creating a second hexagram. Having two hexagrams against which to examine your question will give you much information and enlightenment. In this chapter, we will examine:

- the concept of **changing lines**
- **constructing** a hexagram from one that contains changing lines
- the **secondary hexagrams** that can emerge from this process
- the **nuclear hexagram**

## CHANGING LINES

The idea of changing lines is based on the concept that when yin reaches its maximum it becomes too strongly yin to stay balanced and so it transforms into yang. Likewise, when yang reaches its maximum it becomes too strongly yang to stay balanced and so it transforms into yin. Changing lines are an indication of the possible future, the course you may need to take in the future, or the things of which you will need to be aware. They can be taken as either a warning or an encouragement. Changing lines indicate that your present situation is in a transformative stage.

When you are constructing your hexagram using the coin method (pages 83–84) or the bead method (page 86), you will be noting which lines of your hexagram are affected by a changing or moving line. If you used the coin method, you will note that the hexagram may contain changing lines if you have thrown coins to the value of 6 or 9.

| Throw value | Line | Changing line | Changes to |
|---|---|---|---|
| 6 | Yin | Yes | Yang |
| 7 | Yang | No | |
| 8 | Yin | No | |
| 9 | Yang | Yes | Yin |

When one or more changing lines appear in a hexagram, you can draw a second hexagram derived from the first. The principle is simple. In your second hexagram, all fixed lines from the first hexagram will remain the same. All changing lines from the first hexagram transform into their opposite. Hence changing yin lines turn into fixed yang lines and changing yang lines turn into fixed yin lines.

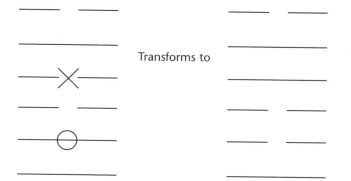

Transforms to

Changing from one hexagram to another

# THE POSITION AND MEANING OF THE CHANGING LINE

Sometimes called its ranking, the position of a changing line can show the hierarchy and status of change. For example, a changing line occurring on the bottom line, or first position, will refer to the beginning of a situation, while a changing line on the top line, or sixth position, looks at the end of a situation.

It is important to consider that the position of yin and yang lines within a hexagram has enormous bearing on the auspiciousness of the whole hexagram. It is the nature of yang to resonate with odd numbers. If a solid yang line is found in the first, third, and fifth lines (the "yang lines") of a hexagram, this is auspicious and is referred to as **yang line correct**. If a yang falls on any of the other lines, it is called "incorrect."

Yin resonates with even numbers and a broken yin line likes to fall in the second, fourth, and sixth positions of a hexagram. If a yin line falls on one of these three lines, the situation is referred to as **yin line correct** and if it does not, this is called "incorrect." If a yin line occupies a yang position, this can mean hesitation or a feeling that you are unequal to the task at hand or that you feel unable to act. If a yang line occupies a yin position, your actions may be too strong for the task at hand.

Remember that each line in a hexagram also has a particular resonance with other lines; there is a relationship between the first and fourth lines, the second and fifth lines, and the third and sixth lines (see pages 92–94).

**POSITION/LINE 1 (BOTTOM POSITION, FIRST LINE):** This represents the beginning of the situation. All possibilities are open. We enter into the situation as a newcomer and need to find our paths and fight for our survival. The first line represents the common people, the collective consciousness, and traditions. It can mean the ignorant and simple person, the untrained worker, the absence of a title, and a very weak influence. It suggests the lowest common denominator.

**Yang line correct:** You have a healthy attitude and are steadfast, well rooted, and trustful.

**Yin line incorrect:** Difficult beginning, poor grounding, and danger.

**POSITION/LINE 2:** A yielding line is preferable in this position. It is the place of minor leadership, of an official in direct relationship with the ruler who holds the similar middle position in the upper trigram on the fifth line. It relates to office managers and public officials with limited power who are still subordinate to higher powers. It is a safe position—if anything goes wrong higher up the ladder, it will not affect you greatly. You will avoid direct conflict with authority. The situation has advanced, but further steps will follow.

**Yin line correct:** You are open to suggestions, flexible in your opinions, open to new contacts, and cheerful.

**Yang line incorrect:** You may suffer from rigid thinking, exaggerated ambitions, and stubbornness.

**POSITION/LINE 3:** This is a place for a firm line. This position is often unfavorable. Usually, the danger in a situation is shown in this line. As this line is partnered with the sixth line, indicating the top of the upper trigram, a changing line in this position may symbolize a situation where there is an attempt to leave the lower trigram (which has a lower ranking and weaker power than the upper trigram).

Transitions, social climbing, and heads of departments are indicated. We can face many dangers and things beyond our control for which we can get blamed. It is the start of the human level, so is the most difficult position. We strive for advancement, taking risks that will either win or fail. This is a crossover point from the lower trigram to the higher one—we are rising in the ranks. The time between jumping and landing can be dangerous. If there is a yin line in the third position, we may be receiving a warning.

**Yang line correct:** You can make clear decisions and feel confident to advance.

**Yin line incorrect:** You may feel too delicate or overtaxed—your nerves are too weak to sustain the effort.

**POSITION/LINE 4:** In the bottom position of the upper trigram, we make the breakthrough we need so that we are now in the inner court (symbolized by the upper trigram), under the gaze of the ruler in the fifth line. This is the place of a minister, high-ranking official, a vice-president, a personal assistant to a very important person, the procurator to the master, an established person, or the upper middle class. The first difficulties have been mastered and you passed the tests. What comes next? You are now in a position of trust. This requires extreme humility and caution because you are close to the highest authority. If anything goes wrong, you are the first person to have your reputation damaged. It is beneficial in the structure of the hexagram for the character of the fourth and fifth lines to be opposite in yin and yang nature so that they are not in conflict.

**Yin line correct:** You are sympathetic, hearty, and open.

**Yang line incorrect:** You should watch out for backbiting. Dangerous forces are opposed to you. However, do not become callous or ill-tempered; maintain your grace and dignity. A warning is implied that you must be cautious in your dealings.

**POSITION/LINE 5:** This is the place of the ruler and should be a yang line. It is in the center of the upper trigram and controls the whole hexagram. The ruler possesses the most superior position in the hexagram. This line represents the head of a family, a CEO, headmaster, king, pope, four-star general, or the principal person in any situation. This line is usually favorable. By the fifth line, the situation has reached its peak or you have realized your natural power before a decline begins. It is beneficial for this line to be opposite in nature to the second and fourth lines so conflict is avoided.

**Yang line correct:** You are at your peak; however, look to the second line for help. Auspicious if it is in yin, as this will bring much-needed assistance to your endeavors.

**Yin line incorrect:** You have reached your peak; however, you still must be on guard. It is of great assistance if the second or fourth line is yang.

**POSITION/LINE 6:** This line represents the great sage who has left the affairs of the world behind—a retired person who has served his or her country well, but still has influence. It is the wise advisor, honorary member, highest spiritual authority, or someone who has left the day-to-day running of a business but is still a board member. It represents a person leaving society or who has already left. Questions of succession emerge.

**Yin line correct:** You feel mentally open and intuitive and are able to listen to spiritual signals.

**Yang line incorrect:** You still feel inappropriately attached to the material world and feel drawn to being manipulative.

# THE PROGRESSED HEXAGRAM

This second hexagram is also known as a progressed hexagram (*zhi gua*), or the **transformed hexagram**. It indicates your future circumstances, whereas the first hexagram indicates your current situation. The progressed hexagram tells you what the short- or long-term results will be. It symbolizes the course you may take in the future or matters you should be aware of.

The position of a changing line can further explain how these changes take place (see pages 92–94), as each position of a changing line has a different interpretation. These interpretations are only a general rule, of course—there are many nuances that may slightly vary this pattern, depending on the question you ask and the type of matter it concerns. Pay particular attention to what happens around the fifth line, as this line is the leader, ruler, or host of the hexagram.

A hexagram can have up to six changing lines. The more changing lines, the more changeable, fluid, and transitional your circumstances are. Many changing lines often indicate rapid changes. The dynamics of the changing lines expand the sixty-four hexagrams into more than four thousand patterns. Since there are sixty-four possible original hexagrams, and each one can change into one of sixty-four final hexagrams, the number of possible combinations is 4,096 (64 x 64).

If a hexagram does not contain any changing lines, the I Ching answer is very definite and specific and the situation you are dealing with is fixed. Where a hexagram has no changing lines, it is called a **locked hexagram**.

## INTERPRETING YOUR PROGRESSED HEXAGRAM

After you have converted the changing lines to form a new hexagram, you will need to assess the meaning of the new hexagram and check the relationships and juxtapositions of its lines. Do the following:

1. For the original hexagram, see the table following its description. This table gives you a brief description of the relevant changing lines. The position of a changing line can show the hierarchy and status of change. For example, a changing line occurring on the bottom line, or first position, will refer to the beginning of a situation, while a changing line on the top line, or sixth position, looks at the end of a situation.
2. Consult the description of the progressed hexagram.
3. If there are no changing lines you will have only one hexagram description to read—the original hexagram (see Chapter Six). No progressed hexagram is created, as there is no change. This can indicate a stable condition or stagnation in your current situation.

## WORKBOOK EXERCISES

1. Imagine that you have asked the question, "Shall I join the committee/club/group as a helper? Let us imagine that you have done a coin casting, producing a hexagram that looks like this:                Your progressed hexagram is:

2. Look up the description of hexagram 16 (see page 125) and check the brief comments about lines 3 and 4 in the table of changing lines on that page. Then read the description of hexagram 15 (see page 124).
3. What does hexagram 16 tell you about your present situation? Note your thoughts in your I Ching journal.
4. What does hexagram 15 tell you about the future? Note your thoughts in your I Ching journal.

## WHICH CHANGING LINE TO READ

The following list indicates additional ways of reading your hexagram if you have changing lines. For clarity, if you have a number of changing lines (which may indicate rapid changes) you will need to know which of these lines is the most important one, as this changing line will often hold the key to your situation.

**For one changing line,** note its advice and also its position. Take note of the hierarchy of lines, such as line 6 being outside the situation or representing spiritual guidance and line 5 being in the position of power (see pages 92–94).

**For two changing lines,** there are only two types of combinations. When they are of the same type, look only at the bottom line. For example, if you have two changing yang lines, read only the lower yang position, as this is the essence of the situation and has the most power here. If one changing line is firm (yang) and one is yielding (yin), look only at the yielding changing line. The yin line shows the inner essence of the situation and therefore has the most meaning.

**For three changing lines,** look only at the central changing line. This follows the Taoist principle of the middle, rather than the beginning or end, being the most important.

**For four changing lines,** the emphasis is on the two unchanging lines. With so much change, the integrity is where there is no change. Of the two stable lines, pay particular attention to the top unchanging line. This polarizes and distances the situation so that we can see it clearly. It is as if we were stepping back and then looking back inside.

**For five changing lines,** look at the only unchanging line. The more changing lines, the more dynamic and dramatic the situation. The line that does not change controls the whole situation.

**For six changing lines,** consult the description of the new progressed hexagram. Do not bother to read any changing lines of the original hexagram, since before you know it they will have changed to their opposites.

# NUCLEAR HEXAGRAMS

Another hexagram can also be derived from the original hexagram. Within each hexagram, there are two nuclear, or "hidden," trigrams, which make up another hexagram. The nuclear hexagram (*hu gua*) is also referred to as the core, mutual, or inner hexagram, and it indicates hidden aspects of your situation. It can show the root of a problem underneath the superficial layers, giving a hint as to the origin of the situation.

To make a nuclear hexagram, remove the outside lines (lines 1 and 6) from the original hexagram. The ancient sages regarded the first and last stage of any situation as weak and unstable. Hence the most vital stage lies in the middle, which leaves you with lines 2, 3, 4, and 5 of the original hexagram. To construct your nuclear hexagram:

• Form the inner "lower nuclear" trigram from lines 2, 3, and 4.
• Form the inner "upper nuclear" trigram from lines 3, 4, and 5.

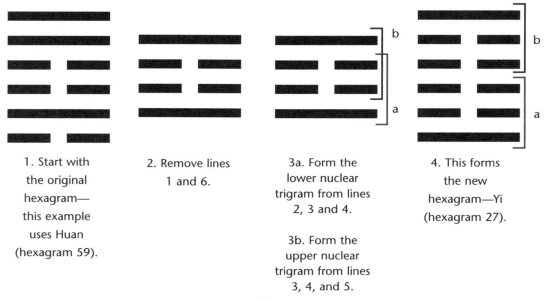

1. Start with the original hexagram— this example uses Huan (hexagram 59).

2. Remove lines 1 and 6.

3a. Form the lower nuclear trigram from lines 2, 3 and 4.

3b. Form the upper nuclear trigram from lines 3, 4, and 5.

4. This forms the new hexagram—Yi (hexagram 27).

## THE CORE HEXAGRAMS

All nuclear hexagrams eventually reduce down to four hexagrams. They reduce to the first two and the last two hexagrams in the sixty-four hexagram sequence—Qian (Heaven, hexagram 1: Initiating), Kun (Earth, hexagram 2: Responding), Ji Ji (hexagram 63: Already Fulfilled) and Wei Ji (hexagram 64: Not Yet Fulfilled), and are referred to as the "core of the core." Each type sheds light on one of the various processes within a full cycle of life according to the I Ching: creation, response, completion, and transition.

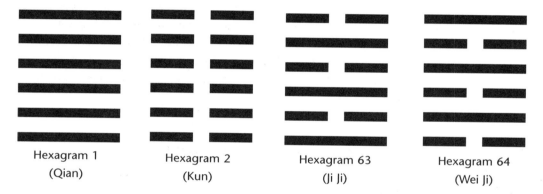

| Hexagram 1 | Hexagram 2 | Hexagram 63 | Hexagram 64 |
| (Qian) | (Kun) | (Ji Ji) | (Wei Ji) |

Apart from the above four core hexagrams (1, 2, 63, and 64), there are twelve other possibilities for nuclear hexagrams. These other possibilities are divided into four groups of three. Each group relates to one of the final reduced hexagrams: 1, 2, 63, or 64. Each group has its own central meaning.

When you have made your nuclear trigrams, put them together to form a new hexagram. Check the table on page 192 and determine the number of your nuclear hexagram. Check the tables on pages 100–102 to see which group your nuclear hexagram fits into.

## THE FOUR CORE NUCLEAR HEXAGRAMS

| Group | Meaning |
|-------|---------|
| 1 | (Initiating) The character is the yang energy, advising you to begin action. |
| 2 | (Responding) The character of this group is yin, advising you to act faithfully and to be steady. Do not rush. |
| 63 | (Already Fulfilled) Its character symbolizes accomplishment and represents skill and a time of success. This situation has occurred through perseverance. However, success can make you complacent. Do not become overconfident. For every great success, there is also some loss. Be respectful and accountable. |
| 64 | (Not Yet Fulfilled) The beginning of a new cycle when everything is in limbo and all lines are incorrectly placed according to their yin and yang nature. But yin and yang are in partnership and matters look promising. This represents transition, from chaos to order again. Keep your promises, be altruistic, and do not be greedy. |

## THE NUCLEAR HEXAGRAM GROUPS

### Group 1

| Nuclear hexagram | Original hexagrams | Meaning |
|------------------|--------------------|---------|
| 28 (Great Exceeding) | 30, 55, 56, 62 | Do not do anything exceeding its limit and good fortune will follow. |
| 43 (Eliminating) | 14, 32, 34, 50 | Five yang lines eliminate yin. Things seem easy at the moment and they are, but do not lower your guard. Be fair. Expose some vulnerability or other yin issue you wish to eliminate. Win by being selfless and virtuous. As the trigrams that make up this hexagram are Lake (delight) over Heaven (creativity), you may be delighted by the end result of a creative venture. |

## Group 1, continued

| Nuclear hexagram | Original hexagrams | Meaning |
|---|---|---|
| 44 (Encountering) | 13, 31, 33, 49 | Yang should not overlook the ever-increasing strength of the yin. The interaction between yin and yang needs to be balanced. |

## Group 2

| Nuclear hexagram | Original hexagrams | Meaning |
|---|---|---|
| 23 (Falling Away) | 3, 8, 20, 42 | It is like autumn when yin energy is increasing. It is better to stay still and not move too much. Protect the inside and guard against decay. In time you will continue to grow, but not yet—the focus is more on inner movement, such as thinking and planning. Fortify the center, such as your soul, and nourish the yin—be gentle with yourself and others. |
| 24 (Turning Back) | 4, 7, 19, 41 | It is better to follow faithfully, actively watch the feminine, and learn your lessons now. These preparations will benefit you in the not-too-distant future. |
| 27 (Nourishing) | 29, 59, 60, 61 | Nourish your body as well as your spirit. The two yang lines are at the extremes, bottom and top, encapsulating the yin in between. It looks like a pot on the stove, suggesting that you may need to nourish yourself and support others. |

## Group 63

| Nuclear hexagram | Original hexagrams | Meaning |
|---|---|---|
| 38 (Diversity) | 5, 9, 48, 57 | In diversity there is still similarity of functions. One needs to study the significance of this and find the common thread in all things. |
| 40 (Relief) | 15, 22, 36, 52 | The thunderstorm is over and the conflict is resolved. Yin and yang harmonize again. The danger is removed. |
| 54 (The Marrying Maiden) | 11, 18, 26, 46 | The oldest son (Thunder) can harm the youngest daughter (Lake). As things do not feel right, you may need to find the middle path and do the right thing. |

## Group 64

| Nuclear hexagram | Original hexagrams | Meaning |
|---|---|---|
| 37 (Household) | 6, 10, 47, 58 | The principle of running a household also lends itself to governing a country. Management is indicated here. Everyone must feel part of the process, with both higher and lower ranks feeling bonded. Be consistent with your good deeds and take responsibility for your actions. |
| 39 (Hardship) | 16, 21, 35, 51 | Water over Mountain suggests the need to be cautious and wise. Observe very closely what is going on. Try to foresee where the difficulty lies. Use divination and seek more advice from trusted friends. |
| 53 (Developing Gradually) | 12, 17, 25, 45 | Be clear and explore the way of progression and advancement. This is the image of the element of Wood growing on the foundation of the Mountain trigram below. It is a sign of marriage, of gradual growth. The wind brings blessings and a promise of success. |

# WORKBOOK EXERCISES

These exercises act as a summary of the concepts to which you were introduced in this chapter. Once you have completed them, try setting your own questions along the same lines.

1. Make a progressed hexagram from the following coin casting. What hexagram do you make?
   - Sixth throw is 6 (yin).
   - Fifth throw is 7 (yang).
   - Fourth throw is 8 (yin).
   - Third throw is 8 (yin).
   - Second throw is 7 (yang).
   - First throw is 9 (yang).

2. A coin casting has yielded the following hexagram. Is this a locked hexagram? Is this a nuclear hexagram?
   - Sixth throw is 8 (yin).
   - Fifth throw is 7 (yang).
   - Fourth throw is 7 (yang).
   - Third throw is 7 (yang).
   - Second throw is 7 (yang).
   - First throw is 8 (yin).

3. Make a nuclear hexagram from this original hexagram. What hexagram do you make?
   - Sixth line is a yang line.
   - Fifth line is a yin line.
   - Fourth line is a yin line.
   - Third line is a yin line.
   - Second line is a yang line.
   - First line is a yin line.

   What is the "feeling" of the nuclear hexagram—can you guess its hidden message?

   What is the name of the lower nuclear trigram, and what is the name of the upper nuclear trigram?

   What family members do the lower and upper nuclear trigrams relate to?

*See page 184 for answers.*

## CHAPTER SIX

# THE SIXTY-FOUR HEXAGRAMS OF THE I CHING

*Learn about each of the hexagrams and what they mean. How to interpret the answers.*

The hexagrams bear much wisdom. Some of the meaning is deeply symbolic and requires much reflection. Each hexagram speaks to all humankind and to the seeker individually. Use this checklist to gain the benefits of consulting the hexagrams of the I Ching.

## STRATEGY FOR READING THE HEXAGRAMS

Here is a useful checklist for a method of conducting an I Ching reading. It includes cross-references to various relevant pages of this workbook to refresh your memory. There are many ways of going about this task. However, by following a ritual each time you consult the I Ching, you will build up a more receptive energy for tuning in. You will ultimately find your own path, but in the meantime consider using the following strategy as one possible way of accessing the wisdom of the I Ching:

1. Find a **space** where you will not be disturbed. Make preparations to help you feel distant from the everyday world (see pages 34–36).
2. Bring into your space your **workbook, I Ching journal, and coins or beads**.
3. **Prepare yourself** for the consultation by conducting a simple meditation (see page 35).
4. Figure out your **question** (see pages 37–41). Write it down in your journal.
5. While thinking of your question, **construct your first hexagram** (see pages 80–88), noting any changing lines. Draw this hexagram in your journal.
6. Take note of the top three lines (the upper trigram) and the bottom three lines (the lower trigram). Use the upper and lower trigrams to **find the number** of your hexagram—use the table on page 192.

7. Look up the **description of this hexagram** (page numbers are given on page 192) and note in your journal any comments that seem relevant to your question. You may also wish to refer to the relevant trigrams contained within your hexagram (see pages 44–79).

8. Check the **relationship between the lines** of the hexagram (see pages 92–94).

9. If your hexagram indicates that some **lines are changing**, also read the table below the hexagram. Refer to pages 90–97 for a description of changing lines. Think of your question. Note in your I Ching journal anything that occurs to you while reading the relevant changing lines. If there are more than two changing lines, figure out which one is the most relevant line (see page 97).

10. In your I Ching journal, **change the relevant changing lines** and keep the unchanged lines of the original hexagram (see pages 95–96). This will give you your progressed hexagram, which will indicate your immediate future.

11. **Check the number of the progressed hexagram** by dividing it into two trigrams and looking at page 192.

12. **Check the description of the progressed hexagram** in Chapter Six. Note in your I Ching journal any comments that may have relevance to the immediate future of your situation.

13. Go back to your original hexagram and construct a **nuclear hexagram** made from the middle four lines of your hexagram. This will help you attain a deeper analysis of the situation (see pages 98–99).

14. **Check the number of the nuclear hexagram** on page 192.

15. Check which **group** your nuclear hexagram falls into. See pages 100–102 for a description of the groups.

16. Note all relevant **comments about the nuclear hexagram** in your I Ching journal.

17. Take some time to **allow the information to filter** through your mind. Draw the original, progressed, and nuclear hexagrams side by side in your journal and gaze at the images. Ask your question again.

18. **Write down your thoughts and impressions**, connecting the information you have gathered from the hexagrams. You may be amazed by the results.

## INTERPRETING THE ANSWER

The sages of the spirit world may sometimes give messages that can be disconcerting or unexpected. Their messages are unpredictable; our questions could be answered at length or we may appear to be given information that is irrelevant to the question. It is difficult for us to understand why a question asked at a certain time does not appear to receive any answer, while at another time it can trigger a long discourse.

The simple answer is that there is a time for everything—sometimes we are simply not meant to know the answers to our questions. To come to understand this, and also to be able to understand what messages the sages are sending, we need to ask heartfelt questions. Only such questions can help us connect with the world of higher consciousness. Tuning into the flow of energy around us (meditation is excellent for this) will enable us to find the right question—the question for which an answer is already waiting.

Interpreting a message from the I Ching is always a highly individual process, one that will become easier with practice. When you have identified the hexagram relevant to you, you will need to make personal symbolic associations in order to link the hexagram's message to the question you have asked. It is important to listen to your intuition without allowing your logical mind to get in the way. Your first thoughts, images, or feelings are often the most true. The fact that the I Ching is not a purely rational system will help you, when seeking enlightenment on situations in your life, to access, value, and take into account your subconscious reading of reality.

When you are reading the text of a hexagram, what matters is not what is written in the text of the I Ching or in this workbook, but what comes up inside you while you read it. Your message may take the form of special images or symbols or a flash of vision apparently unrelated to what is written in the I Ching. You will then need to relate the message to concrete elements in your present situation. There is no fixed code of interpretation; each symbol will have to be reinterpreted each time you consult the I Ching, depending on the situation and the background concerning the question. A symbol may even have completely opposite meanings in two consultations. The only way to achieve skill in consulting the I Ching is to cultivate fluid thinking and to let associations come up freely in your consciousness.

The I Ching is not moralistic—it is not about good or bad. An omen may be auspicious or inauspicious. If you find your answer to be generally inauspicious, it means there is still work to be done and you need to keep seeking the depths of the situation, as issues remain to be uncovered. This is a good time to develop a receptive and reflective quality. The situation is still challenging and this will be a beneficial time to develop yourself.

If the answer is generally auspicious, it can mean that your direction is suitable for you. Keep going and you will find that your path runs smooth. Success will follow. But be aware that everything changes to its opposite.

# GUIDE TO THE HEXAGRAMS

Each hexagram is introduced by the following (hexagram 46 is used as an example here):

1. Number and name: 46, Sheng
2. Core concepts: Pushing upward, ascendance
3. Attributes: Steady growth, increase, arising, spring
4. Overall level of auspiciousness of each hexagram—*This is a sign of a good omen.*

The following table will give you an explanation of the meanings of the various levels of auspiciousness used in each hexagram reading:

| Level of auspiciousness | Meaning |
| --- | --- |
| ★★★ This is an indication of a great omen. | Success will follow you. |
| ★★ This is a sign of a good omen. | Keep doing what you are doing. |
| ★ This is a sign of good fortune. | Keep on your chosen path, but continue to be cautious. |
| ▲ There is nothing to blame. | Whatever is happening, it is not your fault. |
| ✦ Regret will disappear. | Things are changing to the opposite. |
| ✦✦ You may have bad luck. | Be cautious in your actions and thoughts. |
| ✦✦✦ Be very cautious—this is a warning. | Take time for serious reflection; you may need to stop. |

## LINES IN THE HEXAGRAM

As discussed in Chapter Five, the position of yin and yang lines within a hexagram has an enormous bearing on the auspiciousness of the whole hexagram. It is the nature of yang to resonate with odd numbers. If a solid yang line is found in the first, third, or fifth lines (yang lines) of a hexagram, this is auspicious and is referred to as "yang line correct." If yang falls in any of the other lines, it is called "yang line incorrect."

Yin resonates with even numbers and a broken yin line likes to fall in the second, fourth, or sixth positions of a hexagram. If a yin line falls on one of these three lines, the situation is referred to as "yin line correct" and if it does not, this is called "yin line incorrect." If a yin line occupies a yang position, this can mean hesitation, the feeling of being unequal to the task on hand, or the sense of an inability to act. If a yang line occupies a yin position, your actions may be too strong for the task on hand.

In the hexagram, there is also a particular resonance with other lines (see pages 92–94).

Other information you may find useful for interpreting your hexagram:
• The eight trigrams: see pages 44–79.
• Changing lines: see pages 90–97.

## THE SEQUENCE OF LINES IN A HEXAGRAM

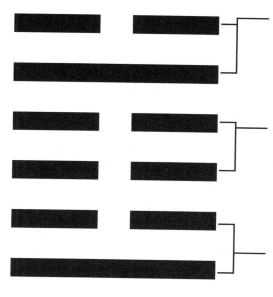

**Lines 5–6** represent heaven or our "third eye." Shows psychological and spiritual influences. Fifth line is usually the ruler of the whole hexagram, as this position signifies the peak between heaven and earth.

**Lines 3–4** symbolize human affairs and the social and emotional aspects of life. Being in the middle, the human can ascend or descend, advance or retreat. Education and self-cultivation can increase the possibility of ascent.

**Lines 1–2** symbolize earth. Represent survival, instinct, and health. Especially significant if your question is about material things.

# 1 QIAN

## THE CREATIVE/THE EMPEROR

*Attributes: Potent yang energy, sublime success*

This hexagram comprises Heaven over Heaven, indicating that you are like an emperor with the potential for power and strength and the ability to achieve your higher goals and visions.

However, it is extremely important that you are virtuous in your intentions and steadfast in your goals and that you make it your paramount responsibility to be receptive and alert to the higher power. It is our destiny to cultivate our heavenly potential fully— failing to do so is contrary to our fundamental drives.

This is an auspicious omen. Once you have attained a broader perspective, you will become prosperous. This hexagram, which relates to the primal energy from which all forms of life emerge, is symbolic of success in new ventures or relationships if you understand the cycle of life, knowing when to put energy into your project or relationship and when not to persist. Take the time to rest and prepare yourself. Be assured that dynamic and creative changes are in motion. In business, you may find that activity is slow and that it is not a good time to commit yourself to long-term plans.

You are strong enough now to achieve your goals—use this strength only in humane, loving, moral, wise, and just ways. If you do, you will achieve sublime success. If you use your strength excessively, or are arrogant or overly ambitious, you will fail and may find yourself caught in a web of corruption; you may also lose opportunities because of complacency and carelessness.

| Line no. | Brief reading for changing line | Level of auspiciousness |
|---|---|---|
| Line 6 | Matters should be humbly left to mature of their own accord. | ✚ Regret will disappear. |
| Line 5 | This is the time to act and take advice. | ★ This is a sign of good fortune. |
| Line 4 | You will succeed after a shaky start if you keep your intentions clear. | ▲ There is nothing to blame. |
| Line 3 | Constant activity and clear thought will enable you to realize your ambitions. | ▲ There is nothing to blame. |
| Line 2 | The time is right to set a goal that you would like to achieve. | ★ This is a sign of good fortune. |
| Line 1 | This is a time for meditation rather than action. | ★ This is a sign of good fortune. |

Overall level of auspiciousness: ★★★ This is an indication of a great omen.

*Heaven trigram: pages 46–49. Changing lines: pages 90–97.*

## 2 KUN

### THE RECEPTIVE, MOTHER EARTH, THE QUEEN

*Attributes: Pure yin energy, the passive principle, receptivity to wise counsel*

This hexagram comprises Earth over Earth, indicating that if you are like Mother Earth and are receptive to the energy of Heaven you will find abundance—in the receptive soil one seed may produce ten thousand seeds. This hexagram represents the primal womb, which gives birth, providing bodily form to new life.

This hexagram urges you to be receptive to guiding influences. Remember that you can yield and be responsive to Heaven's will and still be true to yourself. Choosing your own path or following your own inclinations will not work out well at the moment. Choose to follow another's wise lead, as this will meet with success. But how can you know who are your right friends and mentors? Like the ideal mother, you too must develop unconditional love—a love that is beyond emotional entanglement. You will then be able to accept your friends as they truly are and be in a better position to understand whether what they say and do is wise.

This hexagram advocates a gentle, steady, firm, and courageous approach to your issue. By following this path you may have to wait a little longer than you would like for the desired result, but the wait will be most rewarding. Doing things on impulse will not give you any lasting success. Thinking that you alone must control your decision will only invite disaster—when you try to control everything, everything will go out of control.

| Line no. | Brief reading for changing line | Level of auspiciousness |
|---|---|---|
| Line 6 | Keep your wits about you or matters may be irrevocably spoiled. | ✚ Regret will disappear. |
| Line 5 | You will achieve great success if you remain humble and follow orders. | ★★★ This is an indication of a great omen. |
| Line 4 | You may need to circumvent an issue to avoid further problems. | ▲ There is nothing to blame. |
| Line 3 | Self-discipline and wisdom will bring you success. | ▲ There is nothing to blame. |
| Line 2 | Single-minded action will help you achieve your goal. | ★ This is a sign of good fortune. |
| Line 1 | Have patience and tread carefully. | ★ This is a sign of good fortune. |

Overall level of auspiciousness: ★★★ This is an indication of a great omen.

*Earth trigram: pages 50–53. Changing lines: pages 90–97.*

# 3 ZHUN
## OBSTRUCTION, DIFFICULTY IN THE BEGINNING
*Attributes: The budding of awareness, the processes of learning and becoming clearer*

This hexagram comprises Water over Thunder, which suggests the image of dark clouds before a storm and subsequent heavy rain pouring from the heavens. This may appear to be a time of darkness and disorder, but sooner or later the rain and thunder will stop and the clouds will disperse, resolving chaos and helping things to germinate.

This is a period when new situations are full of potential to develop, so you should devote your energies to careful preparation and timing, and to strengthening your ability to distinguish reality from illusion.

As this is a time of confusion, be watchful for any corrupting influences around you that may divert you from your true path. You are young and innocent at this stage, but do not feel vulnerable, as you must attempt to make order out of disorder. You may need to sever certain karmic links—to untangle entwined destinies or to reassess certain family dynamics—particularly when negativity manifests within the family. You may have to look closely and assess whether you are responding to the illusions created by false learning or social conditioning.

This is not a good time for action. You are advised to put your affairs into proper order and then temporarily disengage yourself. Go with the flow and a good opportunity will eventually present itself.

| Line no. | Brief reading for changing line | Level of auspiciousness |
|---|---|---|
| Line 6 | Matters can only improve from this point. | + Regret will disappear. |
| Line 5 | Your behavior should be governed by consistency and propriety. | + Regret will disappear. |
| Line 4 | Seize a long-awaited opportunity. | ★ This is a sign of good fortune. |
| Line 3 | A current plan should be abandoned rather than stubbornly carried through. | + Regret will disappear. |
| Line 2 | Success is delayed but assured. | + Regret will disappear. |
| Line 1 | Matters should be resolved by an unbiased mediator. | ★ This is a sign of good fortune. |

Overall level of auspiciousness: ★★ This is a sign of a good omen.

*Water trigram: pages 62–65. Thunder trigram: pages 54–57. Changing lines: pages 90–97.*

# 4 MENG
## YOUTHFUL FOLLY, THE EMPTY CUP
*Attributes: Immaturity, inexperience, perplexity, confusion*

This hexagram comprises Mountain over Water, evoking the images of a little spring in the mountains and the purity of a young mind, which is like an empty cup. Character must be developed just as the stream must be directed into strong channels as stable as a mountain.

This is a time in which to acknowledge areas of naïveté, suspend mistrust of the unknown, and allow a more experienced person or expert in the relevant field to lead and instruct. The Mountain represents knowledge and Water the journey. Combined they suggest your pathway to great things—if you know how to be a good student. Develop your modesty and you will find that you will attract the attentions of a great teacher who will be receptive to your needs.

Alternatively, you may be called to guide one younger or less worldly than yourself, in which case you must cultivate within yourself patience, thoughtfulness, and consistency, and within your pupil sincerity and a willingness to learn.

Should your student prove to be overly demanding or psychologically incapable of receiving instruction at this time, you can at least allow your forbearance and kindness to provide the student with a fine role model. In time, this person will outgrow these difficulties.

| Line no. | Brief reading for changing line | Level of auspiciousness |
|---|---|---|
| Line 6 | Ignorance should be corrected rather than punished. | ▲ There is nothing to blame. |
| Line 5 | Useful experience can be won through childlike curiosity. | ★★ This is a sign of a good omen. |
| Line 4 | Ignorance and former errors must be overcome. | ✦ Regret will disappear. |
| Line 3 | Avarice can only lead to ill fortune. | ✦ Regret will disappear. |
| Line 2 | Be tolerant of those who behave foolishly. | ★★ This is a sign of a good omen. |
| Line 1 | Bad behavior demands a reaction, but punishment is not the answer. | ✦ Regret will disappear. |

Overall level of auspiciousness: ★ This is a sign of good fortune.

*Mountain trigram: pages 70–73. Water trigram: pages 62–65. Changing lines: pages 90–97.*

# 5 XU

## CONFIDENT PATIENCE, CALM ABIDING

*Attributes: Waiting, the need for nourishment, calculated inaction*

This hexagram comprises Water over Heaven, which suggests clouds rising to the heavens, eventually to rain and provide nourishment from above. Rain refreshes all that grows and so ultimately provides humankind with food and drink. This gift, however, comes in its own time, rather than at our bidding, and so we must learn to wait for it despite our need. This hexagram requires the development of patience.

Waiting becomes arduous only when we lack confidence that all will occur for the best in its own time. We can learn to endure apparent delays if we have steadfast faith that the future will be bright. When we approach waiting with an inner certainty that our goals will be attainable, the anticipation in itself may be a cause for celebration.

Xu discourages worrying and interference before the time is ripe. Rather, it recommends that we use the fallow time well, preparing ourselves both spiritually and physically. This may mean that we focus on nourishing the body wisely to enrich and complete the soul.

Acceptance of waiting does not mean abandoning ambition. By allowing us to nourish our bodies and spirits, patience strengthens our ability to grasp opportunities.

| Line no. | Brief reading for changing line | Level of auspiciousness |
|----------|--------------------------------|--------------------------|
| Line 6 | The unsought-for assistance of others will further your ambitions. | ★ This is a sign of good fortune. |
| Line 5 | Sobriety during celebrations will benefit you. | ★★ This is a sign of a good omen. |
| Line 4 | Patience and reconciliation will make a tricky situation more bearable. | ▲ There is nothing to blame. |
| Line 3 | Beware of becoming bogged down in time-wasting pursuits. | ✚✚ You may have bad luck. |
| Line 2 | Gossip, though annoying, will not greatly upset your plans. | ★ This is a sign of good fortune. |
| Line 1 | This is a time for patient perseverance in your work. | ▲ There is nothing to blame. |

Overall level of auspiciousness: ★★ This is a sign of a good omen.

*Water trigram: pages 62–65. Heaven trigram: pages 46–49. Changing lines: pages 90–97.*

# 6 SONG

## ANTAGONISM, CONTENTION

*Attributes: Quarrels, disputes, litigation, argumentative natures*

This hexagram comprises Heaven over Water, which suggests a necessary divergence. Heaven's nature is to rise, while water's is to descend. Water parts from heaven as gravity draws rain from clouds, and social harmony is pulled apart by differences of opinion. The inner peace and independence represented by the Heaven trigram is undermined by the heaviness of Water.

Where such divergence of nature or ideas occurs, situations may rapidly turn ugly—unless we remain clearheaded and ready to meet opponents halfway. Rather than personally pushing matters to the limit (even though we may have justifiable cause), it is wise to seek arbitration from an impartial, experienced mediator.

In divination, Song recommends calmness and caution. For example, if the question asked concerns business, any great undertakings are advised against; if marriage is the issue, the prospects are not favorable. Song also advises us to keep a close eye on our tempers.

It should also be remembered that much outer conflict is ultimately a reflection of conflicts within ourselves. Many misunderstandings and arguments can be avoided if we remain true to our inner feelings and reluctant to indulge in anger, self-righteousness, and suspicion.

| Line no. | Brief reading for changing line | Level of auspiciousness |
|---|---|---|
| Line 6 | Impatience and ill-advised arguments may betray your ambitions. | ✚ Regret will disappear. |
| Line 5 | A disagreement can be settled through clear, insightful expression. | ★★★ This is an indication of a great omen. |
| Line 4 | If your position is not strong, an argument is best abandoned. | ★★ This is a sign of a good omen. |
| Line 3 | Your past achievements cannot be stolen from you. | ★★ This is a sign of a good omen. |
| Line 2 | Nothing will be gained from continuing to challenge a stronger foe. | ▲ There is nothing to blame. |
| Line 1 | Leave your emotions out of the current debate. | ★★ This is a sign of a good omen. |

Overall level of auspiciousness: ▲ There is nothing to blame.

*Heaven trigram: pages 46–49. Water trigram: pages 62–65. Changing lines: pages 90–97.*

# 7 SHI

## THE ARMY, COLLECTIVE ENERGY

*Attributes: Gathering your forces, competition, war*

This hexagram comprises Earth over Water. Water is collecting in the ground and, in overabundance, may become a powerful destabilizing force. As Earth in this case represents massed humanity, Shi warns of potential danger to the multitudes.

At a national level, these dangers may be lessened by the existence of a well-ordered and disciplined army. People assembled in an army are powerful, but if poorly trained and led they may be dangerous to themselves. Therefore Shi stresses that the general of the forces must be loyal, experienced, and dedicated to the benefit of all.

In battle the success of an army depends on the degree of trust the soldiers place in their commanders. Since the purpose of military affairs must at all times be righteous, only a person of genuinely noble character should take charge.

Shi often indicates that we should develop our own leadership qualities in our business or social lives, but also encourages us to achieve the correct relationship between the stronger and inferior elements of our personalities. Like an army, our personalities require self-discipline and honorable leadership—in this case, from our higher selves.

| Line no. | Brief reading for changing line | Level of auspiciousness |
|----------|--------------------------------|------------------------|
| Line 6 | Praise and reward those deserving of it. | ✚✚ You may have bad luck. |
| Line 5 | A dishonorable victory is worse than failure. | ✚✚ You may have bad luck. |
| Line 4 | Having made some progress, a temporary retreat is now wise. | ▲ There is nothing to blame. |
| Line 3 | There is a danger of too many cooks spoiling the broth. | ✚✚ You may have bad luck. |
| Line 2 | Treat those beneath you with compassion and respect. | ★ This is a sign of good fortune. |
| Line 1 | Having made up your mind, do not be tempted to change tactics. | ✚✚ You may have bad luck. |

Overall level of auspiciousness: ★ This is a sign of good fortune.

*Earth trigram: pages 50–53. Water trigram: pages 62–65. Changing lines: pages 90–97.*

# 8 BI

## UNION, ASSISTANCE

*Attributes: Accord, alignment, integration, cohesion, support*

This hexagram comprises Water over Earth. The waters of the upper trigram mingle as they traverse the land of the lower trigram, forming streams and rivers until they blend in the ocean, hence Bi's central image of union and mutual help. The five yielding lines of the hexagram hold together because the strong fifth line unites them. The leading position of this line ensures that all may further their truest interests.

As the waters grow strong through union, so do communities. Nothing is more auspicious than harmonious relationships between individuals. To survive and flourish, people must love and care for each other. Our bonds should be as strong as those of a mother and child.

To achieve this we must pay attention not only to those around us but also to our inner selves. Through our mistakes and misunderstandings, we discover the guidelines that make relationships work. We must cultivate a sincere desire for harmony and mutual support in our friendships, communities, and workplaces.

| Line no. | Brief reading for changing line | Level of auspiciousness |
|----------|--------------------------------|-------------------------|
| Line 6 | Be patient and let others make the first move. | ✚ Regret will disappear. |
| Line 5 | Those around you need to understand their roles. | ★★ This is a sign of a good omen. |
| Line 4 | Take advice from someone you hold in high esteem. | ★ This is a sign of good fortune. |
| Line 3 | Do not become part of a poorly planned scheme. | ✚✚ You may have bad luck. |
| Line 2 | Allow your instincts to guide you in your choice of companions. | ★★ This is a sign of a good omen. |
| Line 1 | A sincere desire for the benefit of many in turn benefits you. | ★★ This is a sign of a good omen. |

Overall level of auspiciousness: ★★ This is a sign of a good omen.

*Water trigram: pages 62–65. Earth trigram: pages 50–53. Changing lines: pages 90–97.*

## 9 XIAO XU
### THE TAMING POWER OF THE SMALL, RESTRAINT
*Attributes: Delays, hindrance, quiet accumulation, storing up energy*

This hexagram comprises Wind over Heaven, suggesting the calm movement of clouds across the sky. This indicates that change is possible, but only in relatively insubstantial and fleeting matters. The sole yin line needs time to accumulate strength before lasting results are achievable.

Xiao Xu tells us that our influence is currently limited by external circumstances. Progress appears to have come to a standstill, perhaps in the face of small obstructions brought about by our inexperience. In the face of such delays, we should devote ourselves to rest and preparation. With little ability to exert our influence on external reality, this is a time for refining our inner worlds.

While we might at this time appear overly submissive, thereby discouraging the confidence of others, we can nevertheless make small changes through gentle, friendly persuasion. Self-discipline must be cultivated to prevent ambition from exerting negative pressure.

In all things, this hexagram advises of patience and caution. In business, it recommends preparation for new developments. In relationships and marriage, it warns of temporary trouble and suspicion. It is essential not to compromise our characters in the face of these small tribulations. Great lessons may be learned from small matters.

| Line no. | Brief reading for changing line | Level of auspiciousness |
|---|---|---|
| Line 6 | Others will be unwilling to agree to action at this time, so patience is advised. | ▲ There is nothing to blame. |
| Line 5 | A group effort is more likely to succeed than doing it alone. | ★ This is a sign of good fortune. |
| Line 4 | Confidence and courage grow as you move forward. | ▲ There is nothing to blame. |
| Line 3 | Misunderstandings may occur if emotion and intellect clash. | ✚ Regret will disappear. |
| Line 2 | You and your companions should agree to persevere. | ★★ This is a sign of a good omen. |
| Line 1 | The current path is undoubtedly the best. | ★ This is a sign of good fortune. |

Overall level of auspiciousness: ★ This is a sign of good fortune.

*Wind trigram: pages 58–61. Heaven trigram: pages 46–49. Changing lines: pages 90–97.*

# 10 LU

## FOLLOWING A PATH, TREADING CAREFULLY

*Attributes: Dignified conduct, comportment, taking a risk but watching your step*

This hexagram comprises Heaven over Lake, two forces so greatly separated by the distance between them that no disharmony arises. The lower trigram is likened to a trusting and cheerful daughter finding her way without mistakes by treading in the footsteps of her powerful father, represented by the upper trigram (the word *lu* originally meant "shoes").

The path taken may be unfamiliar and fraught with danger, but with careful planning and sensible precautions harm will be avoided. Where no immediate peril looms, time should be spent considering those dangers that may lie ahead.

The precarious situations alluded to by this hexagram are often of a social nature. Lu advises us to behave with decorum, diplomacy, and good humor, safe in the knowledge that these may pacify even the most irritating of individuals. It suggests that a sufficiently tactful individual might even tread on a tiger's tail without incurring a reprisal, while an aggressive person practically invites the tiger to bite.

This gentleness of nature and consistency of manners may be learned from those whom we like and respect, again as the child may learn the ways of the world by following a wise parent's footsteps.

| Line no. | Brief reading for changing line | Level of auspiciousness |
|---|---|---|
| Line 6 | Your conscience will tell you if your current path is correct. | ★★ This is a sign of a good omen. |
| Line 5 | You should advance despite potential dangers. | ▲ There is nothing to blame. |
| Line 4 | Learning from a mishap will enable you to advance safely. | ★ This is a sign of good fortune. |
| Line 3 | Beware of individuals who are misrepresenting themselves. | ✦✦ You may have bad luck. |
| Line 2 | Advance calmly, confidently, and soberly. | ★★ This is a sign of a good omen. |
| Line 1 | Old ambitions should now be put into action. | ▲ There is nothing to blame. |

Overall level of auspiciousness: ★ This is a sign of good fortune.

*Heaven trigram: pages 46–49. Lake trigram: pages 74–77. Changing lines: pages 90–97.*

# 11 TAI

## PEACE, HARMONY

*Attributes: Contentment, communion, perfect balance, fecundity*

This hexagram comprises Earth over Heaven, a particularly favorable combination. The commingling of earth qi and heaven qi produces a period of tranquillity and fruitfulness. As if this is an idealized country of the imagination, negativity is consistently counterbalanced and transformed by positive energies. The atmosphere is like that of a bright day in the early spring.

In this environment, great ideas and a spirit of compassion and benevolence effectively oust pettiness. Individuals support each other like a mother (Earth) and father (Heaven), all acting in respectful and loving unity. Rising above self-interest, family, friends, and colleagues find it unusually effortless to preserve harmony.

While the time is highly favorable for all projects concerned with communal success, we are encouraged to increase good fortune through the maintenance of our own goodwill and healthy attitudes. These are also easier than usual to achieve since, like the harmony of heaven and earth, our conscious and subconscious minds will be working very compatibly.

The word *tai* is considered highly auspicious in Chinese, hence the hexagram suggests a time when success is easy to come by. Small investments will yield large profits.

| Line no. | Brief reading for changing line | Level of auspiciousness |
|---|---|---|
| Line 6 | Now is the time for maintenance and reparation rather than advancement. | ✚ Regret will disappear. |
| Line 5 | The spirit must be encouraged to govern the body. | ★★★ This is an indication of a great omen. |
| Line 4 | Good-hearted friends will help to buoy up your flagging self-confidence. | ★ This is a sign of good fortune. |
| Line 3 | An unchanged situation may give a sense of peacefulness. | ▲ There is nothing to blame. |
| Line 2 | Kindness to others brings its own reward. | ★ This is a sign of good fortune. |
| Line 1 | Discussing matters will reveal your inner thoughts. | ★★ This is a sign of a good omen. |

Overall level of auspiciousness: ★★ This is a sign of a good omen.

*Earth trigram: pages 50–53. Heaven trigram: pages 46–49. Changing lines: pages 90–97.*

## 12 PI

### STANDSTILL, STAGNATION

*Attributes: Disharmony, contraction, obstruction, adversity, estrangement*

This hexagram comprises Heaven over Earth. While the two trigrams' reversed positions in hexagram 11 indicated a beneficial commingling of Earth and Heaven, here the two are distant and alienated from each other. The result is obstruction and negativity. Where there is strength at the top and weakness below, things can easily collapse; where there is strength without and weakness within, there is only superficiality and fragility.

This sort of skin-deep strength is often found in the sorts of people who come into ascendance in a period associated with Pi. Their public bravado and arrogance is frequently a facade for a very feeble spirit within. In time these weak rulers will be recognized as such and overthrown, but the damage they do often outlives them.

When such individuals dominate, those of more substance are undervalued or disliked and must firmly resist any temptation to sell their integrity for favor or fortune. Further problems are all we can expect to encounter if we permit ourselves to be caught up in false thinking.

In such periods of adversity, Pi reminds us to remain steadfast and remember that all conditions are temporary and that better times must necessarily lie ahead.

| Line no. | Brief reading for changing line | Level of auspiciousness |
|---|---|---|
| Line 6 | Celebrate the end of a period of confusion and disorder. | ▲ There is nothing to blame. |
| Line 5 | A willingness to act gives inner strength. | ▲ There is nothing to blame. |
| Line 4 | Others are grateful for your efforts in maintaining order. | ▲ There is nothing to blame. |
| Line 3 | Your interests need to be put on hold while you aid the common good. | ▲ There is nothing to blame. |
| Line 2 | A firm grip on the situation is called for. | ▲ There is nothing to blame. |
| Line 1 | Group discussions will reveal important secrets and resentments. | ★ This is a sign of good fortune. |

Overall level of auspiciousness: ▲ There is nothing to blame.

*Heaven trigram: pages 46–49. Earth trigram: pages 50–53. Changing lines: pages 90–97.*

# 13 TONG REN

## FELLOWSHIP, GATHERING IN THE FIELD

*Attributes: Comradeship, community, like-minded people, seeking harmony*

This hexagram comprises Heaven over Fire and suggests flames, like human spirits, rising to the heavens as if seeing their reflection in the sun and stars. As individual flames are more easily extinguished than a bonfire, so may the human spirit ascend more powerfully when it is in unity with others.

True community is much more than a mere mass of humanity, and so Tong Ren emphasizes the value of those who have the capacity for leadership and the ability to organize and create a unifying group purpose. Alliances are dependent upon common ground and shared goals and activities. We must be reminded that we all come from the same source and that the sun shines equally upon all.

Among the most potent enemies of community are factionalism, suspicion, and secrecy—hence Tong Ren's title of "Gathering in the Field," a place of openness, both physical and spiritual. Secret reservations and unhelpful attitudes must be brought out into the open where they can be gently and respectfully corrected.

The creation of such communities will not eradicate challenges, but if the group's unity is maintained these can be met bravely with expectations of eventual success.

| Line no. | Brief reading for changing line | Level of auspiciousness |
|----------|--------------------------------|-------------------------|
| Line 6 | A peacekeeper approaches, prepared for strong opposition. | ▲ There is nothing to blame. |
| Line 5 | Good humor helps to defuse volatile confrontations. | ▲ There is nothing to blame. |
| Line 4 | On the brink of advancement, a period of quiet observation is advised. | ★★ This is a sign of a good omen. |
| Line 3 | Underhanded tactics prove useless. | ✚ Regret will disappear. |
| Line 2 | There is no use in having the halfhearted on your side. | ✚ Regret will disappear. |
| Line 1 | The situation resolved, the mediator moves on. | ▲ There is nothing to blame. |

Overall level of auspiciousness: ★★ This is a sign of a good omen.

*Heaven trigram: pages 46–49. Fire trigram: pages 66–69. Changing lines: pages 90–97.*

# 14 DA YOU

## POSSESSION IN GREAT MEASURE, ABUNDANCE

*Attributes: Wealth, vast resources, a great harvest*

This hexagram comprises Fire over Heaven—the Fire above being, naturally, the sun shining over the land, while Heaven below indicates an inner strength with outer clarity. In this radiant situation, obstacles have melted away to allow the manifestation of magnificent prosperity and abundance.

In this atmosphere of clarity, we can confidently do the right things at the right time to ensure a fine harvest. Such bounty, however, will have its drawbacks unless it is accompanied by a commitment to maintain the harmony that initially created this time of prosperity and peace.

The primary danger to which Da You alerts us is the pride that often follows on the heels of success. Arrogance will lose friends, gain enemies, and undermine the foundation of our achievements. Similarly, many have frittered away both their gains and their support through the self-indulgent pursuit of luxuries.

In contrast, remaining humble and generous in the midst of plenty allows for continued growth and increased respect. Wealth and personal power are both increased when these are seen as responsibilities rather than mere possessions. Great success occurs when we are in harmony with the cosmos.

| Line no. | Brief reading for changing line | Level of auspiciousness |
|---|---|---|
| Line 6 | Higher powers appear to be on your side. | ★★ This is a sign of a good omen. |
| Line 5 | A honest and fearless exchange of ideas benefits all. | ★★ This is a sign of a good omen. |
| Line 4 | An inner wisdom will guide you in your actions and timing. | ▲ There is nothing to blame. |
| Line 3 | It is important to align your will to that of a higher power. | ▲ There is nothing to blame. |
| Line 2 | There is a danger of becoming overburdened by responsibility. | ★★ This is a sign of a good omen. |
| Line 1 | A sense of humility should be carefully preserved. | ▲ There is nothing to blame. |

Overall level of auspiciousness: ★★ This is a sign of a good omen.

*Fire trigram: pages 66–69. Heaven trigram: pages 46–49. Changing lines: pages 90–97.*

# 15 QIAN

## HUMILITY, MODESTY

*Attributes: Stability of mind, lack of pretension, propriety*

This hexagram comprises Earth over Mountain. Typically, the mountain looms majestically over the lowly earth—the reversal of this order in Qian indicates the elevation of the humble by virtue of humility itself. Thus Qian elaborates on hexagram 14's warning against arrogance.

Humility is a quality of the mature mind, rather than an innate quality, and so it needs to be cultivated. In the undeveloped mind, boasting often attends ambition, and pride and self-importance follow personal success. We need to be on guard against both these conditions, remaining mindful that even if we climb the highest peak we are still standing on the same earth as all humanity.

Only the genuinely humble are capable of leading effectively, acknowledging that extremes of inequality are the source of discontent. Ostentation, whether conscious or carelessly exhibited through discourtesy and a refusal to curb bad personal habits, ultimately erodes success, while a conscientious devotion to deference, respectfulness, and correctness for their own sakes strengthens all.

Restraining our egos and refusing to be seduced by pride, we are well placed to work well with others, regardless of position, age, or gender. We may, however, need to watch out for people who try to take advantage of our humility for their own ends.

| Line no. | Brief reading for changing line | Level of auspiciousness |
|---|---|---|
| Line 6 | A judicious use of force may be required at this point. | ▲ There is nothing to blame. |
| Line 5 | Your personal integrity will win support. | ★ This is a sign of good fortune. |
| Line 4 | This is a time to listen and learn rather than talk. | ★ This is a sign of good fortune. |
| Line 3 | A decent, honest nature will guarantee success. | ★ This is a sign of good fortune. |
| Line 2 | A genuinely good nature is always recognizable. | ★★ This is a sign of a good omen. |
| Line 1 | The truly successful do not sully themselves with arrogance. | ★★ This is a sign of a good omen. |

Overall level of auspiciousness: ★★ This is a sign of a good omen.

*Earth trigram: pages 50–53. Mountain trigram: pages 70–73. Changing lines: pages 90–97.*

# 16 YU

## ENTHUSIASM, VITALITY

*Attributes: Vigorous action, delight, expression*

This hexagram comprises Thunder over Earth, evoking the image of the first thunderstorms of summer. The crashing sound from the clouds banishes the tensions of a period of relative inactivity, and to the relief of all the earth begins to stir.

Similarly, Yu describes the welling up and release of energy within us, whether self-generated or evoked by the animation and enthusiasm of a great motivator. Like the thunder, this effusive energy acts as the firing of a starting gun or a clarion's call to action.

This exuberance is often accompanied and intensified by celebration, feasting, and music. Leaders, religious and secular, have relied upon these methods to raise the spirits of their people for as long as humanity has existed, ensuring that all share in the festivities and happiness. Such confidence and eagerness also inspire loyalty and diligence in supporters and staff.

Such outpourings of giving and receiving, pleasure, and satisfaction will bring together parties of all sides, clearing away obstacles to the realization of our joint aspirations. United in delight and devotion, the community will embark on great undertakings without fear. The only danger lies in a leader's exploiting this enthusiasm for self-indulgent ends.

| Line no. | Brief reading for changing line | Level of auspiciousness |
|----------|--------------------------------|-------------------------|
| Line 6 | A tendency toward self-indulgence needs to be addressed. | ▲ There is nothing to blame. |
| Line 5 | Past events continue to worry you unnecessarily. | ✚ Regret will disappear. |
| Line 4 | If your triumph is honorably won, your friends will celebrate with you. | ★ This is a sign of good fortune. |
| Line 3 | You have been refusing to listen to your inner guide, but will now do so. | ✚ Regret will disappear. |
| Line 2 | The objects of your ambition are questioned, strengthening your resolve. | ★★ This is a sign of a good omen. |
| Line 1 | Counterbalancing self-gratification becomes a priority. | ✚ Regret will disappear. |

Overall level of auspiciousness: ★ This is a sign of good fortune.

*Thunder trigram: pages 54–57. Earth trigram: pages 50–53. Changing lines: pages 90–97.*

# 17 SUI

## FOLLOWING, ADAPTATION

*Attributes: Appropriate change, leading from behind*

This hexagram comprises Lake over Thunder. As Thunder is associated with movement and Lake with joy, the image suggested is one of quietly rippling wavelets caused by an exuberant power that has humbled itself.

In human terms such joy in movement relates to the way in which a wise leader induces people to follow. To lead well, we must understand our place within a situation and the positions of those who look to us for guidance. We must learn how to serve before we can reliably lead, and how to follow before we can expect followers. Without such knowledge we may be tempted to fall back on coercion and cunning, which will only bring resentment and resistance.

We must also learn when to act and when to refrain from action in order to restore our energy. A long period of relentless excitement will lead to ill fortune. We may experience frustration during periods of enforced rest, but this dissatisfaction can in itself be a strong motivation to great achievement. Conversely, no situation will be truly favorable unless we are able to adapt to it.

However, Sui generally indicates a time of gentle, persistent progress during which errors are easily avoided.

| Line no. | Brief reading for changing line | Level of auspiciousness |
|---|---|---|
| Line 6 | Personal integrity must become second nature. | ▲ There is nothing to blame. |
| Line 5 | To lead others, you must dedicate yourself to serving them. | ★★ This is a sign of a good omen. |
| Line 4 | Your behavior is inspiring the admiration of others. | ▲ There is nothing to blame. |
| Line 3 | Put your faith in someone with a proven track record. | ★ This is a sign of good fortune. |
| Line 2 | There is a danger of trusting someone hopelessly inexperienced. | ✚ You may have bad luck. |
| Line 1 | By freeing yourself from limitations, you win others to your side. | ★★ This is a sign of a good omen. |

Overall level of auspiciousness: ★★ This is a sign of a good omen.

*Lake trigram: pages 70–77. Thunder trigram: pages 54–57. Changing lines: pages 90–97.*

# 18 GU

## DECAY, WORK ON WHAT HAS BEEN SPOILED

*Attributes: Degeneration, corruption, healing, confronting the past*

This hexagram comprises Mountain over Wind, which suggests a low wind being halted in its progress by the mountain's bulk. In turn the blustering air currents destroy the plants at the foot of the mountain. Similarly, in human affairs, lax attitudes create problems, which accumulate and introduce corruption into the community.

Gu advises us to look for such defects in ourselves and in our environment and to take steps to repair the damage at the root so it does not recur. Whether the problems are caused by old bad habits, character defects, or poor organization, unless they are dealt with at the core level the cycle will continue to repeat disastrously.

While this hexagram strongly recommends the turning over of a new leaf, it also advises caution and clear thought both before and after change is implemented. There is no point in change if it sacrifices long-term benefits for short-term gain. Correctly identifying and dealing with areas of degeneration and chaos will, however, clear the way to rebirth and great success.

In business, Gu warns of poorly organized finances; in relationships, conflicts caused by differing temperaments and lifestyles; and in health, troubles from impurities and parasites.

| Line no. | Brief reading for changing line | Level of auspiciousness |
|---|---|---|
| Line 6 | You will achieve great things by acknowledging your spiritual nature. | ▲ There is nothing to blame. |
| Line 5 | Your decisions should be governed by clear thought rather than habit or dogma. | ★★ This is a sign of a good omen. |
| Line 4 | Outmoded behavior must be abandoned if progress is to be made. | ✚ Regret will disappear. |
| Line 3 | Backsliding into old habits may occur, but this will mean only minor lapses. | ▲ There is nothing to blame. |
| Line 2 | Passive bad habits may be as destructive as the active varieties. | ▲ There is nothing to blame. |
| Line 1 | You realize that conformity may become a straitjacket. | ★ This is a sign of good fortune. |

Overall level of auspiciousness: ★ This is a sign of good fortune.

*Mountain trigram: pages 70–73. Wind trigram: pages 58–61. Changing lines: pages 90–97.*

# 19 LIN

## APPROACH, EXPANSION

*Attributes: Prevailing, becoming great, being received, making connections*

This hexagram comprises Earth over Lake, suggesting a lake nestled in high ground as if being nurtured in the protection of a stronger power. Both the depth of the waters and the inexhaustible bounty of the earth betoken the unlimited readiness of the wisest people to sustain and educate others. Lin observes that like children being advised by a firm but kindly parent, we are currently in an excellent position to receive instruction vital to our development.

Sustained by good examples and our willingness to learn, we may become like nature at the beginning of spring: hopeful, steadily flourishing, and able to move forward, toward maximum potency. If we are able to read the signs of the times, this period will be one of steady advancement and expansion.

To make the best of this, we must be constantly vigilant, examining our thoughts and motives for any small errors that might also grow as we progress. With foresight, many obstacles can be warded off before they manifest fully.

Like many other hexagrams, Lin warns us not to fall prey to self-importance and lack of discipline as we observe our progress. We must remain balanced between a trusting obedience to our guides and magnanimity toward others as we protect them.

| Line no. | Brief reading for changing line | Level of auspiciousness |
|---|---|---|
| Line 6 | Your personal integrity guides you to triumph. | ★★ This is a sign of a good omen. |
| Line 5 | Your decisions are based on caution and wisdom. | ★★ This is a sign of a good omen. |
| Line 4 | You approach a perplexing crossroads in your life. | ▲ There is nothing to blame. |
| Line 3 | Trusting your instincts will help you find the correct path. | ▲ There is nothing to blame. |
| Line 2 | Your decision will very soon be proven to be the right one. | ★★ This is a sign of a good omen. |
| Line 1 | The way is clear; only weakness of will can undermine success. | ★★ This is a sign of a good omen. |

Overall level of auspiciousness: ★★ This is a sign of a good omen.

*Earth trigram: pages 50–53. Lake trigram: pages 74–77. Changing lines: pages 90–97.*

# 20 GUAN

## OBSERVATION, CONTEMPLATION

*Attributes: Watching, looking down from above, meditation, mental or physical traveling*

This hexagram comprises Wind over Earth. Just as the wind may freely and widely travel over the earth, Guan advises that our thoughts and perceptions should do likewise. Mental clarity is emphasized, since a wind that carries clouds of dust with it will only obscure that which should be observed.

The shape of the hexagram is reminiscent of traditional Chinese towers, an image that stresses how much more we can see from a high position than from the ground. Likewise, we perceive more with a calm, detached mind than with one embroiled in everyday life. Guan therefore recommends temporary withdrawal in order to study our surroundings and contemplate the future.

At the same time, we must not make the mistake of feeling absent from the situation. Even the watcher from the tower is part of the landscape.

In order to understand the state of affairs, we may be called upon either to travel or to gather information through research. This should in both cases be augmented by meditation. While much is learned from what is seen, the inner flow of life is equally important. We should listen to the unseen and gaze into the spaces between words and between breaths.

| Line no. | Brief reading for changing line | Level of auspiciousness |
|----------|--------------------------------|-------------------------|
| Line 6 | Introspection reveals an inner restlessness. | ▲ There is nothing to blame. |
| Line 5 | You will benefit from paying attention to the experiences of others. | ▲ There is nothing to blame. |
| Line 4 | You will feel strongly drawn to seek the company of those you admire. | ★★ This is a sign of a good omen. |
| Line 3 | You may feel tempted to abandon your journey but are advised not to. | ▲ There is nothing to blame. |
| Line 2 | At the threshold of your goal, you do not feel confident to proceed. | ▲ There is nothing to blame. |
| Line 1 | Your inexperience holds you back, but forward motion is advised. | ▲ There is nothing to blame. |

Overall level of auspiciousness: ▲ There is nothing to blame.

*Wind trigram: pages 58–61. Earth trigram: pages 50–53. Changing lines: pages 90–97.*

## 21 SHI HE

### BITING THROUGH, CORRECTIVE MEASURES

*Attributes: Eradicating obstacles, judging, restoring order, confronting negativity*

This hexagram comprises Fire over Thunder, a combination evoking the lightning accompanying a thunderstorm. This image suggests the way in which nature forces through obstacles and restores imbalances of tension. Shi He advises that in human affairs problems should likewise be illuminated with the lightning flash of clear insight and shaken apart by the thunder of unleashed energy.

The shape of Shi He also suggests an open mouth (the yang lines on the top and bottom being the lips) with something in it (line 4). *Shi* means "to bite" and *He* means "to close"—action to remove obstacles is reinforced by the image of biting through the obstruction.

In society such eradication of disorder must be governed by an effective and honorable justice system. Legal arguments are also suggested if the obstacle in the mouth is thought of as words that need to be spoken. The law must be properly administered if social harmony is to prevail. Punishment is sometimes required but must be appropriate to the crime and free from vindictiveness.

Shi He often portends a legal action or the appearance of a third party in a marriage or relationship, causing a disruption that will diminish in the face of patience.

| Line no. | Brief reading for changing line | Level of auspiciousness |
|----------|--------------------------------|-------------------------|
| Line 6 | You may be unaware of the approach of danger. | ✚✚ You may have bad luck. |
| Line 5 | Despite the perils, courage and perseverance will arm you well. | ▲ There is nothing to blame. |
| Line 4 | Cautious perseverance will reap rewards. | ★★ This is a sign of a good omen. |
| Line 3 | Progress is impeded by obstacles and doubts, but all is far from lost. | ▲ There is nothing to blame. |
| Line 2 | A goal too easily achieved brings its own dangers. | ▲ There is nothing to blame. |
| Line 1 | An approaching danger may seem inescapable, but to be forewarned is to be forearmed. | ▲ There is nothing to blame. |

Overall level of auspiciousness: ★ This is a sign of good fortune.

*Fire trigram: pages 66–69. Thunder trigram: pages 54–57. Changing lines: pages 90–97.*

## 22 BI
### GRACE, ADORNMENT
*Attributes: Glamour, elegance, glow, presentation*

This hexagram comprises Mountain over Fire. This suggests the just-rising sun at dawn or the low-setting sun at dusk, or a bonfire at the foot of the mountain illuminating and emphasizing its beauty. There is great value and inspiration to be taken from such natural beauties, although we must remain careful not to perceive surface appearances only—we must remember to see beyond superficialities.

Appreciation of beauty inclines us toward harmony and precision rather than chaos and carelessness. Whenever our aesthetic sensibilities urge us to adorn nature or society, this should be focused solely on abiding value and importance.

Such guidelines often seem admirable in theory but fail in practice. In ourselves, overemphasis on surface beauty can eclipse our natural grace, leading to reckless and unfair judgments, pretense, and bravado.

We must maneuver carefully and thoughtfully—do not be dazzled by surface appearances, but assess the true ramifications of the situation. In particular, beware of taking legal matters lightly.

Contemplation of the resplendency of form is enriching, but we must not take its permanency for granted. Its fleeting nature instructs us in the nature of time and being and so reveals the beauty of the spirit and the worlds behind this world.

| Line no. | Brief reading for changing line | Level of auspiciousness |
|---|---|---|
| Line 6 | Simplicity and honesty bring your goal within reach. | ▲ There is nothing to blame. |
| Line 5 | Practicality and freedom from ostentation make success achievable. | ★ This is a sign of good fortune. |
| Line 4 | Those who genuinely earn the respect of others rarely try too hard. | ★ This is a sign of good fortune. |
| Line 3 | To the heart, inner beauty outshines all surface glitter. | ★★ This is a sign of a good omen. |
| Line 2 | Your values allow you to rise above the world of appearances. | ★ This is a sign of good fortune. |
| Line 1 | Abandoning vanity brings about liberation and furthers your quest. | ★ This is a sign of good fortune. |

Overall level of auspiciousness: ★ This is a sign of good fortune.

*Mountain trigram: pages 70–73. Fire trigram: pages 66–69. Changing lines: pages 90–97.*

## 23 PO

### SPLITTING APART, DISINTEGRATION

*Attributes: Decay, fragmentation, collapse from within, falling away*

This hexagram comprises Mountain over Earth. A mountain standing alone on the earth is exposed to the elements and will in time be worn down by erosion and landslides. Similarly, all our achievements will eventually be prone to forces of disintegration.

The shape of the Po hexagram suggests weakness rising from within. Specifically, it resembles a house splitting apart, held together only by the roof (the top line). Dark inferior forces gradually undermine what is superior, so that collapse is inescapable. There is little support and no strength within.

When such conditions take hold, no action or intervention proves useful. We should not attempt to postpone the inevitable, but should use the time for patient planning and consolidation. We must view the adversity dispassionately and derive every possible lesson from the situation to avoid repeating mistakes. In business, it is a good time to be careful, work hard, and wait for better times.

Remaining conscious that it is darkest before the dawn, we should hold on to hope and also the certainty of improvement. To prepare for the new beginning, those with knowledge should pass it on to those with less and those with money and power should be aware of their responsibility to help others.

| Line no. | Brief reading for changing line | Level of auspiciousness |
|---|---|---|
| Line 6 | Misfortune ends and the time approaches for new seeds to be sown. | ✚ Regret will disappear. |
| Line 5 | This is a time for submission rather than opposition. | ★★ This is a sign of a good omen. |
| Line 4 | The tide of ill fortune has peaked but still disturbs your peace. | ✚✚ You may have bad luck. |
| Line 3 | You have fallen in with a bad crowd and need to regain your freedom. | ★★ This is a sign of a good omen. |
| Line 2 | You need to face your current problems alone. | ✚✚ You may have bad luck. |
| Line 1 | Peace is being undermined by selfishness and gossip. | ✚✚ You may have bad luck. |

Overall level of auspiciousness: ✚ Regret will disappear.

*Mountain trigram: pages 70–73. Earth trigram: pages 50–53. Changing lines: pages 90–97.*

## 24 FU

### THE TURNING POINT, RETURN

*Attributes: Resurgence, renewal, cycles, fresh beginnings*

This hexagram comprises Earth over Thunder. This suggests an awareness of renewed vitality, represented by the energizing thunder over the sleeping earth. For this reason, Fu is associated with the winter solstice, the day after which the hours of sunlight increase. Although the weather remains cold and desolate, the seeds of warmth and light are beginning to grow.

The promise of revival implicit in hexagram 23 starts to actualize in Fu. The cycle of existence moves steadily toward a better future and so we need not push matters at this time. Transformation of the old comes easily and forward motion continues without obstruction but it moves at its own pace. We must cultivate wisdom and patience as these new adventures unfold.

All new beginnings must be treated with special care, and like someone returning to health after illness, we must not allow impetuosity to impede our progress. As matters move naturally toward success, we should prepare ourselves so that we can make the best of the new opportunities.

In matters of business, this hexagram suggests a slow period that will give way to great success in time. In relationships and marriages, it indicates that although a previous partnership has been unsuccessful, the next will be much more rewarding.

| Line no. | Brief reading for changing line | Level of auspiciousness |
|---|---|---|
| Line 6 | Persistence in a mistaken path threatens long-term consequences. | ✚✚ You may have bad luck. |
| Line 5 | Reparations must be made to correct past mistakes. | ▲ There is nothing to blame. |
| Line 4 | You must choose your own path and for a time walk it alone. | ★ This is a sign of good fortune. |
| Line 3 | Move confidently forward rather than dithering. | ▲ There is nothing to blame. |
| Line 2 | Now is a favorable time to follow others' good examples. | ★★ This is a sign of a good omen. |
| Line 1 | You need to backtrack slightly to correct a small error of judgment. | ★★★ This is an indication of a great omen. |

Overall level of auspiciousness: ★ This is a sign of good fortune.

*Earth trigram: pages 50–53. Thunder trigram: pages 54–57. Changing lines: pages 90–97.*

# 25 WU WANG

## INNOCENCE, PROPRIETY

*Attributes: Correctness, integrity, simplicity, absence of expectations*

This hexagram comprises Heaven over Thunder. Thunder represents natural energy, so Wu Wang suggests the regenerative life force of a burgeoning springtime, which is blessed by the heavens above.

The creators of the I Ching saw only virtue in the expression of such energy, believing such primal innocence to be perfectly attuned to the will of heaven. Summoning this primal purity from our hearts helps to cleanse our overly complicated minds and guide us safely through life.

A major part of this innocence is the state of living in the present. When we spend too much time calculating the results of our labor or seeking approval from others, we can undermine our efforts. We work best when we are fully present in the moment, not when we are distracted by expectations. Forethought is a proper part of our labors, but we can never foresee every eventuality. Wu Wang advises us to adapt to unexpected difficulties should they arise rather than cluttering our minds with possibilities that may never happen.

When our thoughts are free from uncertainty, we can more closely reflect the natural flow of life's energy. Guided by a blend of adult wisdom and the unclouded awareness of a child, we can progress with peace of mind and playfulness.

| Line no. | Brief reading for changing line | Level of auspiciousness |
|----------|--------------------------------|--------------------------|
| Line 6 | This is a time for introspection and stillness rather than action. | ▲ There is nothing to blame. |
| Line 5 | Allow time and nature, not external aid, to heal you. | ▲ There is nothing to blame. |
| Line 4 | Your personal integrity will help prevent misfortune. | ▲ There is nothing to blame. |
| Line 3 | Misfortune or theft may befall someone undeserving of it. | ✚ Regret will disappear. |
| Line 2 | Work undertaken with impatience for results rarely satisfies. | ★★ This is a sign of a good omen. |
| Line 1 | Pure motives will bring about great success. | ★★ This is a sign of a good omen. |

Overall level of auspiciousness: ★★ This is a sign of a good omen.

*Heaven trigram: pages 46–49. Thunder trigram: pages 54–57. Changing lines: pages 90–97.*

## 26 DA XU (DA CHUI)
### THE TAMING POWER OF THE GREAT, APPROPRIATE RESTRAINT
*Attributes: Accumulation, containment, holding firm, potential*

This hexagram comprises Mountain over Heaven, which suggests the vast, creative power of heaven being stored within the stronghold of a mountain. This repository of power may be expressed through the creation of reserves in the bank, the amassing of personal virtue on a daily basis, and the accumulated knowledge, wisdom, and virtuous examples of great individuals in human history.

All these various resources need to be gathered with restraint and firmness, resulting in the inner strength and outer stillness of stored treasure within a mountain cavern. A resolute nature is needed to prevail against the obstacles that great endeavors necessarily encounter. A farmer will find his mettle tested in taming an unruly bull to plow his fields.

Similarly, we need to focus our minds and wills vigorously and decisively in order to succeed in building up our reserves. Much work lies ahead, calling for self-discipline and strong leadership.

Among the hindrances of which Da Xu warns is interference from troublesome people. In such cases, friendships should be cultivated if possible, since such alliances are also great resources. If, for example, the parents of the person one wishes to marry oppose the union, they should be won over by gentle persistence.

| Line no. | Brief reading for changing line | Level of auspiciousness |
|---|---|---|
| Line 6 | The way is clear before you and success awaits. | ★ This is a sign of good fortune. |
| Line 5 | Danger is defused by altering its cause. | ★★ This is a sign of a good omen. |
| Line 4 | Forethought and action prevent a problem from arising. | ★★ This is a sign of a good omen. |
| Line 3 | Skill and courage will see you through a challenging journey. | ★ This is a sign of good fortune. |
| Line 2 | Self-control and restraint are called for. | ▲ There is nothing to blame. |
| Line 1 | Action can only lead to misfortune at this point, so be patient. | ▲ There is nothing to blame. |

Overall level of auspiciousness: ★★ This is a sign of a good omen.

*Mountain trigram: pages 70–73. Heaven trigram: pages 46–49. Changing lines: pages 90–97.*

# 27 YI

## NOURISHMENT, THE CORNERS OF THE MOUTH

*Attributes: Nurturing, caring for oneself and others, temperance*

This hexagram comprises Mountain over Thunder. The invigorating energy of nature symbolized by thunder is felt at the foot of the mountain, ready to rise up and encourage the renewed growth of the various plants that can sustain and heal us. This image of nourishment is also reflected by the hexagram's shape, which resembles an open mouth, the yang lines at top and bottom being the lips.

Happiness depends on being well nourished, both literally and metaphorically. Yi emphasizes that we must take responsibility for both types of self-nourishment. We must put the right food into our bodies and the right types of ideas into our minds and spirits. An emotional or intellectual diet of delusions, fantasies, self-pity, or greed is quite as damaging as unhealthy eating.

Likewise, when we are called upon to nourish others—physically, mentally, and emotionally—we must be careful to discriminate between the pure and the unworthy.

The mouth not only takes in food and drink, but also gives forth speech. Yi stresses that moderation and tranquillity are as important in our words as in our diet. Excess, carelessness, and poor ingredients should be avoided in both cases.

| Line no. | Brief reading for changing line | Level of auspiciousness |
|---|---|---|
| Line 6 | Others may temporarily resent your assistance but you should persevere. | ★ This is a sign of good fortune. |
| Line 5 | Your uncertainty is an obstacle but sound advice will strengthen you. | ★ This is a sign of good fortune. |
| Line 4 | You may need to hunt for those who can be of assistance. | ▲ There is nothing to blame. |
| Line 3 | Question whether your lifestyle is providing spiritual sustenance. | ✚ Regret will disappear. |
| Line 2 | Failing to provide for yourself will undermine your self-esteem. | ✚✚ You may have bad luck. |
| Line 1 | Your spiritual diet, like your physical diet, must be tailored to your specific needs. | ✚✚ You may have bad luck. |

Overall level of auspiciousness: ▲ There is nothing to blame.

*Mountain trigram: pages 70–73. Thunder trigram: pages 54–57. Changing lines: pages 90–97.*

# 28 DA GUO (TA KUO)

## THE PREPONDERANCE OF THE GREAT, THE TENSION OF EFFORT

*Attributes: Excessive pressure, great heaviness, the danger of collapse*

This hexagram comprises Lake over Wind. The I Ching sees this as an image of the waters of a flooding lake rising into the upper branches of the trees that are usually the domain of the wind. Such a condition is unusual and may prove dangerous if we remain in the vicinity.

This worrisome image is reinforced by the hexagram's appearance, which suggests a wooden beam that is thick in the middle (the four yang lines) but weak at both ends (the bottom and top yin lines). The entire roof is likely to collapse once the pressure of the beam's weight causes the weakened ends to give way.

Da Guo advises that the best course at this time is simply to move away as quickly as possible. The direction of the flight is of small importance as long as we clear out of the area of danger.

The excessive pressure that threatens us may have been caused by our ambitions exceeding our abilities or our resources being spread too thinly. In business it may show overexpansion, which has created a shortage of funds and unrest in the workplace.

Either way, success is still attainable if we rise to the occasion. If we act decisively, with courage and self-discipline, all will be well. Our only truly dangerous error at this point would be inaction.

| Line no. | Brief reading for changing line | Level of auspiciousness |
|---|---|---|
| Line 6 | The waters are rising around you but the correct path is still forward. | ▲ There is nothing to blame. |
| Line 5 | Failure to treat others as equals proves unproductive. | ▲ There is nothing to blame. |
| Line 4 | Working for a common good will bring success. | ★ This is a sign of good fortune. |
| Line 3 | You endanger yourself by refusing the support of others. | ✚ Regret will disappear. |
| Line 2 | Renewal is possible through respectful treatment of those beneath you. | ▲ There is nothing to blame. |
| Line 1 | You are advised not to proceed without a safety net. | ▲ There is nothing to blame. |

Overall level of auspiciousness: ★ This is a sign of good fortune.

*Lake trigram: pages 74–77. Wind trigram: pages 58–61. Changing lines: pages 90–97.*

# 29 KAN
## THE ABYSS, THE PERILOUS PIT
*Attributes: Danger, descent, mastering pitfalls, darkness*

This hexagram comprises Water over Water. An overabundance of water will push downward, its weight encouraging the natural tendency of the element to permeate structures. Thus these structures can be undermined and made hazardous. On the one hand, Kan relates to the depths of doubt and desperation, but on the other it suggests that our best strategy for survival at such times is to be like water ourselves: consistent, dependable, and able to move with the currents.

The types of dangers against which the hexagram warns seem extremely daunting: robbery, burglary, deceit, entrapment, abandonment, incapacitation, alcohol abuse, and hazards around water itself.

However, it is also stressed that danger, correctly approached, may indeed bring us benefits. Its proximity sharpens our minds and senses, and by learning to surmount it we can emerge much stronger.

The key to prevailing over such trials is to remain calm and establish a positive attitude. External competence in the face of danger flows naturally from inner mastery, while faith in ourselves ties the heart to life and provides the strength to endure. This is the worst possible time to be overpowered by grief or to take refuge in escapism. Through decisive action we will emerge to safety.

| Line no. | Brief reading for changing line | Level of auspiciousness |
|----------|-------------------------------|------------------------|
| Line 6 | Major rethinking is required to disentangle yourself from problems. | ✚✚ You may have bad luck. |
| Line 5 | Overly ambitious plans have resulted in dangers you must escape. | ▲ There is nothing to blame. |
| Line 4 | Formality should be replaced with directness and integrity. | ▲ There is nothing to blame. |
| Line 3 | Patience, rather than advancing or retreating, is your only option. | ✚ Regret will disappear. |
| Line 2 | Small victories amid problems are all that you can hope for. | ▲ There is nothing to blame. |
| Line 1 | You must remain part of the solution, not part of the problem. | ✚✚ You may have bad luck. |

Overall level of auspiciousness: ★ This is a sign of good fortune.

*Water trigram: pages 62–65. Changing lines: pages 90–97.*

# 30 LI

## BRIGHTNESS, THE CLINGING

*Attributes: Cohesion, illumination, brilliance*

This hexagram comprises Fire over Fire, suggesting both the constant splendor of sunlight above the shorter-lived luminance of terrestrial blazes and the spirits of exemplary humans. As flames cling to their source of fuel and light embraces the surfaces it reveals, so human wisdom attaches to and brightens our lives.

Fire depends on an enduring inner source of nourishment if it is to be sustained. Often, it is difficult to maintain the fires of our enthusiasms due to our failure to supply ourselves with the right amounts of the right sort of fuel, such as inspiration and support. The flames either die away or blaze out of our control.

Li reminds us that in nature each living substance has found a way to survive. With patience and docility we can relearn this instinctive knowledge and move toward a more enlightened state. In business, this hexagram can also indicate that things will get brighter.

Everything we need to know is accessible through the subconscious mind. Once unveiled, this enlightenment can be put to the service of others, illuminating their paths and revealing hope. In this quest for enlightenment we must be wary of becoming fixated with illumination of the self. Nothing of value is produced by vanity and a lack of empathy and compassion for others.

| Line no. | Brief reading for changing line | Level of auspiciousness |
|---|---|---|
| Line 6 | To defuse a situation, attack the source rather than the symptoms. | ▲ There is nothing to blame. |
| Line 5 | Problems must be handled bravely and with dignity. | ★★ This is a sign of a good omen. |
| Line 4 | Unreasonable emotional outbursts will lose you support. | ➕➕ You may have bad luck. |
| Line 3 | Accepting the inevitable with good grace is preferable to complaining. | ➕➕ You may have bad luck. |
| Line 2 | Your behavior is an inspiration to others. | ★★★ This is an indication of a great omen. |
| Line 1 | Composure and concentration are needed to start a project properly. | ▲ There is nothing to blame. |

Overall level of auspiciousness: ★ This is a sign of good fortune.

*Fire trigram: pages 66–69. Changing lines: pages 90–97.*

# 31 XIAN (HSIEN)
## MUTUAL INFLUENCE, COURTSHIP
*Attributes: Attraction, stimulation, sensitivity, support*

This hexagram comprises Lake over Mountain. The lake atop the mountain symbolizes a yin influence that helps to keep a powerful yang force responsive and flexible. At the same time, the lake is supported and raised above what would otherwise have been its humbler station.

In human terms, this beneficial interdependence is most clearly illustrated by well-matched couples who, free from selfishness and prejudice, balance each other's extremes of yin and yang nature. (It should be remembered in this context that yin qualities are not exclusive to women or yang to men.)

Mutual attraction typically arises from two individuals recognizing in each other both similarities and complementary qualities. Tenderness and loyalty are required if the attraction is to transcend seduction and become courtship and eventual bonding. Lasting beneficial associations are only possible when both parties are treated fairly and respectfully by each other.

Xian evokes both the energy and stimulation of new romance and the commitment and joy of newlyweds. The path opens before us and great benefits are attracted into our lives. In our relationships, successful marriages may be indicated, with children soon to follow. Similarly, business dealings are highly favorable, with employers and employees working harmoniously and expansion being imminent.

| Line no. | Brief reading for changing line | Level of auspiciousness |
|----------|--------------------------------|--------------------------|
| Line 6 | Sweet talk and idle conversation will accomplish nothing. | ▲ There is nothing to blame. |
| Line 5 | Your efforts are being sabotaged by your lack of commitment. | ▲ There is nothing to blame. |
| Line 4 | The heart sees more clearly than a cluttered mind. | ✚ Regret will disappear. |
| Line 3 | Impatience may lead to poor timing. | ✚ Regret will disappear. |
| Line 2 | Stillness is called for until a clear indication for action is given. | ▲ There is nothing to blame. |
| Line 1 | Your intentions remain unnoticed until put into action. | ▲ There is nothing to blame. |

Overall level of auspiciousness: ★ This is a sign of good fortune.

*Lake trigram: pages 74–77. Mountain trigram: pages 70–73. Changing lines: pages 90–97.*

# 32 HENG

## PERSEVERANCE, CONSTANCY

*Attributes: Steadiness, continuance, marriage, long-term partnerships*

This hexagram comprises Thunder over Wind, both of which are impermanent forces that nevertheless recur eternally. They therefore suggest that what endures does so by remaining active rather than stagnant. Perseverance is possible through the orderly change exemplified by the changing seasons, rather than stasis.

The I Ching sees thunder as vigorous and wind as gentle, so the combination of these aerial powers also relates specifically to the way in which enduring forces alternate between periods of expansion and contraction, just as we survive through the duality of inhalation and exhalation.

In human terms, Heng follows on from the courtship aspects described by hexagram 31, evoking the notion of long and successful marriages. Where two people love and respect each other and work together with a united purpose, the relationship becomes self-contained and self-renewing. Inner gentleness and outer strength balance each other, creating a powerful and abiding foundation. Through all changes, they remain as constant in their course as the sun and moon.

In business and any other endeavors of importance, Heng advises us to persist in the strategies we know to be appropriate and ethical. We should resist the temptation to try easier methods of operation or to act with disloyalty and self-interest.

| Line no. | Brief reading for changing line | Level of auspiciousness |
|---|---|---|
| Line 6 | Impatience and inner turmoil betray your project. | ✚ Regret will disappear. |
| Line 5 | You need a clear understanding of when to act and when to remain still. | ✚✚ You may have bad luck. |
| Line 4 | Make sure a goal is attainable before spending your energy on it. | ✚ Regret will disappear. |
| Line 3 | Inconsistent behavior does little for one's reputation. | ✚ Regret will disappear. |
| Line 2 | There is no shame in failing to achieve the impossible. | ▲ There is nothing to blame. |
| Line 1 | All successful work consists of successfully accomplished details. | ✚ Regret will disappear. |

Overall level of auspiciousness: ★ This is a sign of good fortune.

*Thunder trigram: pages 54–57. Wind trigram: pages 58–61. Changing lines: pages 90–97.*

# 33 DUN (TUN)
## RETREAT, DISENGAGEMENT
*Attributes: Withdrawal, dignity, self-control, refusal to be provoked*

This hexagram comprises Heaven over Mountain. The image suggests a mountain looming skyward in an attempt to challenge the supremacy of heaven. Heaven, however, retreats rather than being drawn into such competition.

Dun advises that at times when opposing darkness rises against us, the correct and honorable course is retreat rather than engagement. The skill we must learn is to recognize when such withdrawal is appropriate. Cowardice is not to be encouraged, but neither are obstinacy and belligerence when we would only exhaust ourselves and put our endeavors and colleagues in unnecessary danger.

At such times a constructive retreat is far wiser than allowing ourselves to be goaded into failure or to compromise with the encroaching darkness. Pride is the chief obstacle to such tactical withdrawal, so we must guard against it. Disengagement may seem distasteful at times, but is an entirely proper course if we disengage in order to prepare for a counteroffensive once situations are more favorable. We must keep our cool, allowing ourselves to be ruled not by hatred but by a sense of proportion, dignity, and prudence.

Unsurprisingly, Dun warns that this is an unpropitious time for launching new enterprises or embarking on new romances, relationships, or marriages.

| Line no. | Brief reading for changing line | Level of auspiciousness |
|---|---|---|
| Line 6 | A situation can be abandoned with a clear conscience and good spirits. | ★ This is a sign of good fortune. |
| Line 5 | An amicable parting of ways is indicated. | ★ This is a sign of good fortune. |
| Line 4 | You may need to absent yourself from loved ones temporarily to follow your true path. | ▲ There is nothing to blame. |
| Line 3 | A departure is made uncomfortable through insecurity and clinging. | ★ This is a sign of good fortune. |
| Line 2 | The dependency of others may slow down your departure. | ▲ There is nothing to blame. |
| Line 1 | Refraining from action is the best course to avoid confrontation. | ✚ Regret will disappear. |

Overall level of auspiciousness: ★ This is a sign of good fortune.

*Heaven trigram: pages 46–49. Mountain trigram: pages 70–73. Changing lines: pages 90–97.*

# 34 DA ZHUANG (TA CHUANG)
## THE POWER OF THE GREAT, INCREASING STRENGTH
*Attributes: Ascending energy, responsible use of force*

This hexagram comprises Thunder over Heaven, suggestive of the rising movement of storm clouds and, more generally, increasing power (*da* means "great" and *zhuang* means "strength"). The combination of thunder's motion and heaven's strength is reflected in the hexagram's appearance. The four yang lines suggest ascending power, as if the wholly yang lower trigram is extending its influence into the upper.

Da Zhuang's message is the opposite of the preceding hexagram's suggestion of withdrawal. It states that this is a suitable time for positive advancement when our energy is like that of an adventurous young man eager for action. The challenge is to develop the right type of strength and to know what to apply it to.

Excessive force and overconfidence are dangers in such periods. Flexibility, openness to advice, resilience, and perseverance are all requirements of effective power. Without sensitivity and moral integrity, the most powerful person is unlikely to create fruitful results. The truest power is seen in those who possess it but do not wield it carelessly or unnecessarily.

In business dealings, Da Zhuang emphasizes ethical strategies. In relationships, it warns against precipitant action (such as an impulsive marriage proposal). More will be gained through patience and consistent kindness.

| Line no. | Brief reading for changing line | Level of auspiciousness |
|---|---|---|
| Line 6 | There is no point in continuing to beat your head against a brick wall. | ★ This is a sign of good fortune. |
| Line 5 | Now that a situation has been tamed, there is no need for continued aggression. | ▲ There is nothing to blame. |
| Line 4 | Quiet perseverance in your work will lead to success. | ★★ This is a sign of a good omen. |
| Line 3 | Do not expend all your energy too soon. | ✚✚✚ Be very cautious—this is a warning. |
| Line 2 | As problems are mastered, you must beware of overconfidence. | ★★ This is a sign of a good omen. |
| Line 1 | Resist the urge to act too quickly. | ✚ Regret will disappear. |

Overall level of auspiciousness: ★ This is a sign of good fortune.

*Thunder trigram: pages 54–57. Heaven trigram: pages 46–49. Changing lines: pages 90–97.*

## 35 JING (CHIN)
### PROGRESS, ADVANCEMENT
*Attributes: Recognition, promotion, reward, rapid and easy change*

This hexagram comprises Fire over Earth. This evokes the image of the sun effortlessly rising above the horizon at dawn. The ascending sun suggests new beginnings and bright hope for the future, and so Jing announces a period of surprisingly easy progress and ever-widening expansion. Delays have been banished and we are finally presented with an opportunity to fulfill a goal.

Jing also stresses that it is proper for us to emulate the rising sun, allowing our work and talents to help illuminate each other's paths. This is only possible when we keep our motives pure. Just as struggle often consolidates character, progress requiring little effort may undermine it.

Therefore, the cultivation of self-awareness is strongly advised. Our light must not become clouded by insincerity or vanity. When we find success easily, it is not uncommon to slip into pride or self-indulgence. These must be avoided, as must the tendency to put on airs or facades, or to rest on our laurels.

Business prospects are very favorable at this time, with new careers or promotions easily attainable. Relationships are equally positive, and Jing also suggests that this is a fortunate time in which to move to a new house or even a new part of the country.

| Line no. | Brief reading for changing line | Level of auspiciousness |
|----------|-------------------------------|------------------------|
| Line 6 | Keep your temper and treat those working with you respectfully. | ★ This is a sign of good fortune. |
| Line 5 | Great success is possible without resorting to force or arrogance. | ★★ This is a sign of a good omen. |
| Line 4 | Your current course could bring unwelcome secrets into the light. | ✚✚✚ Be very cautious—this is a warning. |
| Line 3 | You are strongly supported by those with faith in you. | ✚ Regret will disappear. |
| Line 2 | Persevere in trying to make connections with those who can help you. | ▲ There is nothing to blame. |
| Line 1 | Despite your doubts, doing what is right will achieve progress. | ▲ There is nothing to blame. |

Overall level of auspiciousness: ★★ This is a sign of a good omen.

*Fire trigram: pages 66–69. Earth trigram: pages 50–53. Changing lines: pages 90–97.*

# 36 MING YI (MING I)

## THE DARKENING OF THE LIGHT, THE WOUNDING OF BRIGHTNESS

*Attributes: Obscurity, adverse conditions, concealment of virtue*

This hexagram comprises Earth over Fire, suggesting the gathering of night as the sun sinks below earth's horizon. Just as hexagram 35 indicates that times of easy progress are part of life's cycle, Ming Yi reminds us that darkness is as inevitable as the dawn.

During such periods, further advancement is exceedingly difficult (although the imagery of night and eventual daybreak indicates that success is achievable when the correct time comes). The wisest course is to hold back, restore energy, and patiently await sunrise and continued progress.

In dark times individuals of an equally dark nature are often found in positions of authority. Ming Yi advises that now is not the time to oppose such people directly or even to shine forth in defiance, since such action could lead to our being swallowed by the darkness. In some situations, we need to conceal our inner light in order to prevail.

This does not mean lending our power to the wrong person or scheme. Instead, we must cultivate outward detachment and inward perseverance. In this way we remain poised between dangerous outspokenness and harmful deceit and may continue to be a living light in the darkness.

| Line no. | Brief reading for changing line | Level of auspiciousness |
|----------|--------------------------------|-------------------------|
| Line 6 | Opposing forces overcome you but will soon lose ground. | ✚ Regret will disappear. |
| Line 5 | Be resolute in the face of mounting opposition. | ★ This is a sign of good fortune. |
| Line 4 | Observe your opponents carefully, looking for weaknesses. | ▲ There is nothing to blame. |
| Line 3 | After an easy victory, beware of implementing change too soon. | ★ This is a sign of good fortune. |
| Line 2 | You suffer a setback but can safely retreat to build up your resistance. | ★ This is a sign of good fortune. |
| Line 1 | Ensure that a single-minded desire for results does not alienate you from others. | ▲ There is nothing to blame. |

Overall level of auspiciousness: ▲ There is nothing to blame.

*Earth trigram: pages 50–53. Fire trigram: pages 66–69. Changing lines: pages 90–97.*

# 37 JIA REN (CHIA JEN)
## THE HARMONIOUS FAMILY, THE WELL-ORDERED HOUSEHOLD
*Attributes: Family relationships, teamwork, communication within a group, leading by example*

This hexagram comprises Wind over Fire. Just as the warming of a house requires heated air that rises from a well-tended fire, the members of the household are comforted and strengthened by the words (wind) that arise from the inner spirit (fire) of each member.

These internal flames must be as carefully maintained and fueled as those in the hearth. Inadequate firewood will produce little warmth and the family will not feel inclined to gather at the hearth. Likewise, words without substance will fail to unite individuals.

Jia Ren emphasizes that integrity and communication are vital to a well-ordered family and therefore to a harmonious society and a peaceful world. Traditionally, an orderly family was founded on the formal, complementary roles and duties of the father, mother, and children. Despite social change, these hold true as metaphors. For example, the roles of men and women are less rigidly defined now, but each individual, family, and group needs a healthy balance of yin and yang qualities.

In the same way, each person involved in an enterprise needs to know how he or she can best contribute. Those who function as leaders must inspire others by cultivating within themselves love, faithfulness, and correctness.

| Line no. | Brief reading for changing line | Level of auspiciousness |
|---|---|---|
| Line 6 | All benefit from the progress you make through good-hearted labor. | ★★ This is a sign of a good omen. |
| Line 5 | Loyalty is achieved through encouraging affection, not fear. | ★★ This is a sign of a good omen. |
| Line 4 | Great success is achieved through prudence and maintaining balance. | ★★★ This is an indication of a great omen. |
| Line 3 | An overly severe and serious nature may undermine success. | ✚ Regret will disappear. |
| Line 2 | Gently correct imbalances in your diet and health. | ★ This is a sign of good fortune. |
| Line 1 | All must understand their role in the community and be respected for it. | ▲ There is nothing to blame. |

Overall level of auspiciousness: ★ This is a sign of good fortune.

*Wind trigram: pages 58–61. Fire trigram: pages 66–69. Changing lines: pages 90–97.*

# 38 KUI (KU)
## OPPOSITION, DISHARMONY
*Attributes: Polarization, cross-purposes, incompatibility, estrangement, inner conflict*

This hexagram comprises Fire over Lake. The nature of flames is to rise and the nature of water is to descend, so the Fire and the Lake have no foundation for achieving the harmony described by hexagram 37. Even the nuclear hexagrams reflect the opposition of the two elements.

In human terms, this lack of communication may be expressed as mere indifference (the water cannot extinguish the flames, nor the flames heat the water) or a more destructive refusal to agree to disagree.

Alerting us to this tendency, Kui recommends trying to reconcile the opposing forces, regardless of whether they involve our own inner disunity, a disagreement with another person or group, or discord between two other parties. The key is to seek harmony through diversity, but we are warned that we will need an appropriate location and correct timing to enable this enterprise to flourish.

If we are a party to the conflict, reflection on our attitudes is necessary. Could our failure to get along with friends and family be due to a misunderstanding or our resistance to change? In contrast, when our motives and information are correct, we must not let ourselves be influenced detrimentally by contrary energies such as fear.

| Line no. | Brief reading for changing line | Level of auspiciousness |
|----------|--------------------------------|-------------------------|
| Line 6 | Mistakenly mistrusting the good-hearted leads to isolation. | ★ This is a sign of good fortune. |
| Line 5 | Beware of misjudging someone who means you well. | ▲ There is nothing to blame. |
| Line 4 | Your isolation will be lessened through the meeting of a kindred spirit. | ▲ There is nothing to blame. |
| Line 3 | Through strength of will you triumph after a dire beginning. | ★ This is a sign of good fortune. |
| Line 2 | An accidental encounter leads to the forging of a strong bond. | ▲ There is nothing to blame. |
| Line 1 | Do not attempt to settle the current challenges through force. | ▲ There is nothing to blame. |

Overall level of auspiciousness: ▲ There is nothing to blame.

*Fire trigram: pages 66–69. Lake trigram: pages 74–77. Changing lines: pages 90–97.*

# 39 JIAN (CHEN)
## OBSTRUCTION, INTERRUPTION OF FLOW
*Attributes: Obstacles, troubles, hardship, impasse*

This hexagram comprises Water over Mountain, suggesting a body of water being held atop a peak. Its natural inclination to flow downhill is impeded. Only when water has accumulated enough volume will it burst free. As it does so it may present new dangers, descending as a powerful, potentially destructive waterfall or as impassable rapids.

Jian warns that our situation has become so fraught with obstacles that it has become extremely dangerous. These external perils—dangers that exist outside you, rather than dangers caused by your attitudes or ideas—should not be confronted directly. If there is any possibility of safely skirting the hazards, it should be taken, but it is more probable that we will need to stay where we are until we have built up our strength and consolidated support. The situation is not one from which we can extricate ourselves. We will need instead to join forces with like-minded companions.

While waiting for the proper time, opportunity, and support, it is important not to fall into self-pity or to cast about for someone or something to blame. It is far better to reflect on whether the difficulty we face is in some measure of our own making. Possibly, the outward danger has been awoken by obstructions within our own thoughts.

| Line no. | Brief reading for changing line | Level of auspiciousness |
|----------|--------------------------------|-------------------------|
| Line 6 | Perseverance will lead to more problems, but resist the temptation to give up. | ★ This is a sign of good fortune. |
| Line 5 | Friends will rally around to support you in your efforts. | ▲ There is nothing to blame. |
| Line 4 | As opposition mounts, take time to gather support and form strategies. | ✚ Regret will disappear. |
| Line 3 | Retreat is more useful than further wasting of energy. | ★ This is a sign of good fortune. |
| Line 2 | A noble sense of duty impels you to continue in the face of opposition. | ✚ Regret will disappear. |
| Line 1 | Analyze the problems blocking you rather than charging into battle. | ★ This is a sign of good fortune. |

Overall level of auspiciousness: ▲ There is nothing to blame.

*Water trigram: pages 62–65. Mountain trigram: pages 70–73. Changing lines: pages 90–97.*

# 40 JIE (HSIEH)
## DELIVERANCE, LIBERATION
*Attributes: Release of tension, convalescence, relief, alleviation*

This hexagram comprises Thunder over Water, suggesting the release of tension after a thunderstorm. Thunder (the Arousing) denotes movement up and away, while Water (the Abysmal) suggests danger. Therefore Jie is the hexagram of movement out of danger—the opposite of hexagram 39.

As the storm dissolves obstacles, difficulties are resolved and advancement is again possible. However, Jie advises us not to relax prematurely or to assume that we can now forge on to major victories. Instead, it recommends that we return as rapidly as possible to our normal way of life and a position of centrality. Our deliverance at this point is no more than a chance to begin anew.

As we move forward toward safety, we must liberate our minds and emotions from the past difficulties. However, unresolved issues need to be addressed before we can let go of the past and allow our future to unfold. If recent difficulties were caused by the misdeeds of others, we should try to forgive them, rather than weighing ourselves down with grievances. Failure to do so will only impede our own progress.

In business, Jie heralds expansion after a difficult period. Those seeking new positions will do well if interviewed in the early morning.

| Line no. | Brief reading for changing line | Level of auspiciousness |
|---|---|---|
| Line 6 | Bold action is required to remove a persistent obstacle. | ★ This is a sign of good fortune. |
| Line 5 | Avoid association with those whose attitudes drain your energy. | ★★ This is a sign of a good omen. |
| Line 4 | Differentiate your true friends from those who wish to exploit you. | ★★ This is a sign of a good omen. |
| Line 3 | Complacency will lead to loss. | ✚ Regret will disappear. |
| Line 2 | You are able to see through the flattery and lies of others. | ★ This is a sign of good fortune. |
| Line 1 | Having cleared the air, you are able to continue easily toward your goal. | ▲ There is nothing to blame. |

Overall level of auspiciousness: ★★ This is a sign of a good omen.

*Thunder trigram: pages 54–57. Water trigram: pages 62–65. Changing lines: pages 90–97.*

# 41 SUN
## DECREASE, RESTRAINT
*Attributes: Cutting back, letting go of what is unnecessary, self-discipline*

This hexagram comprises Mountain over Lake. As energy is constantly redistributed, resources decrease in one area to bring about increase elsewhere. The mountain slowly crumbles into the lake, increasing its size; the water in turn, held in place by the mountain, evaporates.

Sun suggests that when the lowly decreases to the benefit of the upper, stability is more easily undermined than when the flow is reversed. For instance, a building with upper walls that are stronger than the lower is precariously poised, as is a nation in which the ruler's wealth consistently increases as the poor grow more destitute. One of our great challenges is to learn how to manipulate resources without causing instability.

Inevitably, however, all will now and then encounter circumstances that call for great frugality. At such times we must govern our emotions as well as our self-indulgences. Impatience and anger at such reversals of fortune will only impoverish our tranquillity as well. Acceptance and a sense of perspective will avoid the exhaustion caused by resentment. A spiritually harmonious quality of life should be developed to counterbalance material loss.

In both business and relationships, Sun warns against profligacy. Self-restraint is called for to avoid further depletion of both finances and emotional energy.

| Line no. | Brief reading for changing line | Level of auspiciousness |
|---|---|---|
| Line 6 | Real success is achieved through helping, not diminishing, others. | ★★ This is a sign of a good omen. |
| Line 5 | Success is virtually inevitable at this point. | ★★ This is a sign of a good omen. |
| Line 4 | By correcting your errors you make yourself more approachable. | ▲ There is nothing to blame. |
| Line 3 | Be wary of jealousy on the one hand and isolation on the other. | ▲ There is nothing to blame. |
| Line 2 | To be truly of assistance to others you must not weaken yourself in the giving. | ★ This is a sign of good fortune. |
| Line 1 | Be tactful and respectful when assisting those in need. | ▲ There is nothing to blame. |

Overall level of auspiciousness: ★★ This is a sign of a good omen.

*Mountain trigram: pages 70–73. Lake trigram: pages 74–77. Changing lines: pages 90–97.*

# 42 YI

## INCREASE, ACCUMULATION

*Attributes: Material gain, blessings, windfalls*

This hexagram comprises Wind over Thunder, a symbol of increase from above as the wind carries the invigorating sound of the thunder further than it would otherwise go. Yi has the opposite connotations to hexagram 41. Here, generosity is expressed from above, as in a nation where the wealthy work toward decreasing inequality, and all benefit.

Just as the negativity of the previous hexagram is of finite duration, so is the bounty of Yi. Consequently, this is not a time in which to sit idly. Great undertakings are currently well within our potential to bring to fruition. Gain will be increased further through strong, confident action.

While capitalizing on our material good fortune, we must also remember to work on self-improvement, learning from the good examples of others and eradicating the less honorable aspects of our personalities. In our quest to make the most of such beneficial times, we must always act with generosity. Exploiting others for personal gain diminishes the spirit in ways that cannot be offset by external wealth.

In both business and emotional issues, Yi presses us to face challenges, even in the face of friends' apprehension. In this climate of good fortune, we must seize the moment.

| Line no. | Brief reading for changing line | Level of auspiciousness |
|---|---|---|
| Line 6 | Refusal to assist others will lose you respect. | ✚✚ You may have bad luck. |
| Line 5 | Treat others with kindness and with no thought of reward. | ★★ This is a sign of a good omen. |
| Line 4 | You are trusted by all to see that benefits are appropriately distributed. | ✚ Regret will disappear. |
| Line 3 | Cultivate the ability to find blessings in misfortunes. | ★★ This is a sign of a good omen. |
| Line 2 | Nothing can oppose you as long as you value the common good. | ★★ This is a sign of a good omen. |
| Line 1 | Pass on the assistance given to you to others in need of help. | ★★★ This is an indication of a great omen. |

Overall level of auspiciousness: ★★ This is a sign of a good omen.
*Wind trigram: pages 58–61. Thunder trigram: pages 54–57. Changing lines: pages 90–97.*

# 43 GUAI (KUAI)
## BREAKTHROUGH, RESOLVE
*Attributes: Confrontation, determination, speaking out, elimination of unworthiness*

This hexagram comprises Lake over Heaven. Once the waters of the lake have risen to heaven as vapor, looming clouds begin to fill the sky, creating tension that will only be released through heavy rain. Likewise, accumulated water on high ground needs little encouragement to burst through the barriers holding it.

In human affairs this violent discharge of energy is seen when, having been surrounded by dangerous presences, we are forced to resolve them by confronting and eliminating them. Guai advises that the time for hesitation has passed and that the current climate is favorable for tackling these negative forces and influences. Since confrontation is unavoidable, we are counseled to decide how to deal with the situation before it reaches its danger point.

When we are required to deal with such matters, it is important not to fight fire with fire, using our opponents' dishonorable methods against them. Compromising our virtue by using unethical behavior or excessive force or allowing our anger or egos to take the upper hand must be scrupulously avoided.

Guai emphasizes that the wisest tactic in overcoming negativity in others or ourselves is to channel our energies into the furtherance of virtue rather than the overpowering of vice.

| Line no. | Brief reading for changing line | Level of auspiciousness |
|---|---|---|
| Line 6 | An apparent victory may turn sour unless you pay close attention. | ✚✚ You may have bad luck. |
| Line 5 | Small, relentless problems must be faced with diligence. | ▲ There is nothing to blame. |
| Line 4 | You are pushing ahead alone when you would do better to work with others. | ✚ Regret will disappear. |
| Line 3 | Despite a lack of appreciation, you should continue on your path. | ▲ There is nothing to blame. |
| Line 2 | If you remain vigilant, danger will not catch you unaware. | ▲ There is nothing to blame. |
| Line 1 | Gauge your strength before undertaking your next project. | ▲ There is nothing to blame. |

Overall level of auspiciousness: ▲ There is nothing to blame.
*Lake trigram: pages 74–77. Heaven trigram: pages 46–49. Changing lines: pages 90–97.*

# 44 GOU (KOU)
## COMING TO MEET, TEMPTATION
*Attributes: Encountering bad influences, deception, seduction, addiction, dissipation*

This hexagram comprises Heaven over Wind, an image suggestive of heavenly wisdom being disseminated by the freely ranging breeze. Whether this advice is heeded is up to us.

The form of the hexagram suggests the nature of the message. The single yin line can be thought of as infiltrating the otherwise solidly yang hexagram, like darkness gradually taking hold after the apparent victory of light. For this reason, Gou is associated with the summer solstice—the turning point of the year after which daylight lessens and night lengthens.

The heavenly advice that we need to heed is that we must be on guard against unworthy people, influences, and habits. At this point these appear to be harmless, but if their influence is left unchecked the negativity may swiftly and unexpectedly consume us and adversely affect those around us. The kinds of pernicious forces against which Gou warns may easily lead to an addiction to drugs, alcohol, unhealthy food, damaging sexual behavior, gambling, and countless other self-indulgences.

Just as the night's lengthening after the summer solstice is initially almost imperceptible, so can the quietly gathering strength of these seductive inclinations take us by surprise, leaving us in a weakened state and vulnerable to exploitation. This hexagram alerts us to such dangers.

| Line no. | Brief reading for changing line | Level of auspiciousness |
|---|---|---|
| Line 6 | Refrain from impatience at what you consider the foolishness of others. | ▲ There is nothing to blame. |
| Line 5 | Develop a kind, protective attitude toward those in your care. | ▲ There is nothing to blame. |
| Line 4 | Do not alienate those who you find unhelpful. | ✚✚ You may have bad luck. |
| Line 3 | Do not collaborate with those whose motives seem unworthy. | ▲ There is nothing to blame. |
| Line 2 | Use diplomacy rather than force to control problematic people. | ▲ There is nothing to blame. |
| Line 1 | Do not allow your opposition to grow in strength. | ▲ There is nothing to blame. |

Overall level of auspiciousness: ✚ Regret will disappear.

*Heaven trigram: pages 46–49. Wind trigram: pages 58–61. Changing lines: pages 90–97.*

# 45 CUI (TSUI)

## GATHERING TOGETHER, COMMUNITY

*Attributes: Congregating, shared intention, group cohesion, accord, organization*

This hexagram comprises Lake over Earth, which suggests gathering in two ways. First, the lake forms by the accumulation of water from rain and streams. Second, when the waters threaten to rise too high, the community gathers to prevent flooding by reinforcing or raising the enclosing banks. Cui therefore represents the coming together of a large group of people for a shared purpose.

While the collective strength of united communities is capable of effecting great positive changes in the world, there is always the danger of conflict, theft, and exploitation in any crowded situation. Cui reminds us to be prepared for unexpected situations and to work toward keeping order. Like the waters of the lake, the exuberance of the gathering must be safely contained.

Consequently, when a crowd gathers, the stabilizing influence of sound leadership is necessary. To be effective in this role we must develop a firmness of character needed to cope with unforeseen events, remind the assemblage of their mutual intention, and coordinate activity.

Winning the support and trust of our community tests our mental and emotional strength and physical endurance, but when great things are achieved through the goodwill and mutual support of a community, such efforts are richly rewarded.

| Line no. | Brief reading for changing line | Level of auspiciousness |
|---|---|---|
| Line 6 | An offer of friendship seems to have been rejected but may later be realized. | ▲ There is nothing to blame. |
| Line 5 | Be wary of those who feign friendship for favor. | ▲ There is nothing to blame. |
| Line 4 | When you work for a common benefit, envy will not trouble you. | ★ This is a sign of good fortune. |
| Line 3 | A social group seems closed to you but someone will assist you if you allow it. | ▲ There is nothing to blame. |
| Line 2 | Follow your instincts in choosing those with whom to associate. | ★ This is a sign of good fortune. |
| Line 1 | Progress can be made if you join with others for a common purpose. | ▲ There is nothing to blame. |

Overall level of auspiciousness: ★★ This is a sign of a good omen.

*Lake trigram: pages 74–77. Earth trigram: pages 50–53. Changing lines: pages 90–97.*

# 46 SHENG

## PUSHING UPWARD, ASCENDANCE

*Attributes: Steady growth, increase, arising, spring*

This hexagram comprises Earth over Wind. As Wind is also associated with the element Wood, Sheng is suggestive of the gentle, steady, and unceasing growth of a young tree flourishing in early spring. Just as well-nourished saplings reach upward untiringly and with no apparent effort, so will we find movement from a lower level to a higher level easily achievable at this time. Obstacles will be few, minor, and far between.

We are advised to make the most of these favorable conditions, but also to allow our progress to be gradual and unhurried. Like the tree, our growth is assured, although it is not instantaneous. Impatience and haste are usually symptoms of our anxiety about our advancement, but Sheng reassures us that this is a period during which such doubts are baseless. However, also like a burgeoning plant, we should not pause in our activity. Success will be achieved if we continue to move forward with faith and confidence.

In order to continue this harmonious progression, we are counseled to cultivate our willpower and self-control, since the only possible obstructions currently are those that arise internally, such as pride and idleness.

All new undertakings are very favorable at this point, from new business ventures to marriages or conceiving a child.

| Line no. | Brief reading for changing line | Level of auspiciousness |
|---|---|---|
| Line 6 | The most direct path is not always the correct one, so consider alternatives. | ▲ There is nothing to blame. |
| Line 5 | Do not be dazzled by your small successes, but calmly focus on your true goal. | ★ This is a sign of good fortune. |
| Line 4 | Encouraged by someone influential, you continue your steady ascent. | ★ This is a sign of good fortune. |
| Line 3 | All goes well but your luck may soon change. | ▲ There is nothing to blame. |
| Line 2 | A small, sincerely given offering outweighs a greater one given lightly. | ▲ There is nothing to blame. |
| Line 1 | An unshakable sense of rightness will guide you in your quest. | ★★★ This is an indication of a great omen. |

Overall level of auspiciousness: ★★ This is a sign of a good omen.

*Earth trigram: pages 50–53. Wind trigram: pages 58–61. Changing lines: pages 90–97.*

# 47 KUN
## EXHAUSTION, OPPRESSION
*Attributes: Collapse of effort, depression, despair, resignation, restriction*

This hexagram comprises Lake over Water. This suggests a lake from which the water has entirely drained away, sinking beneath the earth or coursing away downhill. This in turn evokes the way we feel when prolonged adversity depletes our energy and confidence.

A sense of purpose is one of our most valuable assets. When it is depleted, progress is not only impossible but also ceases even to seem desirable. Kun reminds us that we all encounter such periods of life from time to time. Our worth is not measured by our success or failure but by our ability to respond to both with grace.

Self-pity and pessimism, even when events appear to warrant them, are invariably dangerous, miring us more deeply in despair when we ought to be concentrating on regaining control. Remaining cheerful in the face of reversals, poverty, and oppression is essential if solutions are to be found. It also encourages others to feel optimistic.

As with an exhausted body, rest and nourishment replenishes a depleted spirit. Kun suggests we use these adverse times to study and engage in research to revitalize our interest in life and prepare the way for future progress. Changes in our work or lifestyles may also be indicated.

| Line no. | Brief reading for changing line | Level of auspiciousness |
|---|---|---|
| Line 6 | Decisiveness is necessary if you wish to succeed. | ★★ This is a sign of good fortune. |
| Line 5 | Despite a lack of human help, the higher powers are with you. | ✚ Regret will disappear. |
| Line 4 | Obstructions and social awkwardness may result from indecision. | ✚ Regret will disappear. |
| Line 3 | Retreat and dependency would be disastrous at this point. | ✚✚ You may have bad luck. |
| Line 2 | External luxury fails to satisfy the soul. | ▲ There is nothing to blame. |
| Line 1 | Guard against surrender to depression and inaction. | ✚ Regret will disappear. |

Overall level of auspiciousness: ▲ There is nothing to blame.

*Lake trigram: pages 74–77. Water trigram: pages 62–65. Changing lines: pages 90–97.*

# 48 JING (CHING)
## THE WELL, THE SOURCE

*Attributes: Replenishment, slaking spiritual thirst, communion, connection*

This hexagram comprises Water over Wind, although the I Ching again uses Wind's association with the element Wood in its imagery. Wood descending into Water suggests the symbol of a well into which poles bearing ceramic bowls (in the traditional Chinese style of well) or wooden buckets (in Western wells) were lowered in order to access the drinking water necessary to a community's existence.

The well in turn suggests the source of that which sustains our spirits. As surely as our bodies need clean water, our spiritual thirsts must also be satisfied. The metaphorical water to nourish the spirit, like the actual water of a well, is located beneath the surface of our lives. Jing reminds us that when we live purely in the superficial order of the world, our deepest needs remain unfulfilled.

If a well is poorly maintained or allowed to become tainted, no one will drink from it. We are therefore reminded by this hexagram to see that our means of attaining spiritual nourishment is kept in good condition.

Jing also relates the well to education, another inexhaustible source of replenishment for all. We should no more neglect our thirst for uncontaminated wisdom and knowledge than our need for water.

| Line no. | Brief reading for changing line | Level of auspiciousness |
|---|---|---|
| Line 6 | Good fortune to all has been achieved. | ★★★ This is an indication of a great omen. |
| Line 5 | Worldly success is dependent upon a well-nourished spirit. | ▲ There is nothing to blame. |
| Line 4 | Now is a good time for spiritual self-examination and balancing. | ▲ There is nothing to blame. |
| Line 3 | An obvious source of sustenance is being overlooked. | ▲ There is nothing to blame. |
| Line 2 | Problems arise from your failure to cultivate your best qualities. | ✚✚ You may have bad luck. |
| Line 1 | Stagnation must be overcome by spiritual renewal. | ✚ Regret will disappear. |

Overall level of auspiciousness: ✚✚ You may have bad luck.

*Water trigram: pages 62–65. Wind trigram: pages 58–61. Changing lines: pages 90–97.*

# 49 GE (KO)

## REVOLUTION, MOLTING

*Attributes: Radical change, innovation, reformation, renewal, upheaval*

This hexagram comprises Lake over Fire. The idea of a fire beneath the surface of a lake immediately suggests opposing tendencies. The lake will attempt to extinguish the fire and the fire will try to dry up the lake. This mirrors life's constant rebalancing of opposites such as yin and yang, summer and winter, and light and darkness.

When imbalances occur, radical changes are sometimes necessary. Like the molting of an animal's fur at the change of seasons, an old order must be abolished to make way for the new. In the political world, this may be expressed through revolutions, as it was many times throughout the history of the Chinese dynasties.

Just as a political revolution manifests itself in the mind before manifesting in the outer world, so all radical changes in our lives must arise after careful consideration. All alternatives must be weighed up, as if we were farmers formulating strategies to cope with both rain and drought.

Even after such deliberation, we must still wait for the most auspicious time at which to act. Ge reminds us that to garner full support the virtues of changes must not be implemented hastily. Effective change requires astute timing.

| Line no. | Brief reading for changing line | Level of auspiciousness |
|---|---|---|
| Line 6 | Having succeeded in great matters, do not neglect the remaining details. | ▲ There is nothing to blame. |
| Line 5 | Your strategies have won the trust of those around you. | ★ This is a sign of good fortune. |
| Line 4 | Great changes can be achieved as long as your motives are pure. | ★★ This is a sign of a good omen. |
| Line 3 | A middle way must be found between hesitancy and impatience. | ▲ There is nothing to blame. |
| Line 2 | Radical change is necessary but must be well thought out. | ★ This is a sign of good fortune. |
| Line 1 | Be absolutely sure whether major changes are necessary before proceeding. | ▲ There is nothing to blame. |

Overall level of auspiciousness: ★ This is a sign of good fortune.

*Lake trigram: pages 74–77. Fire trigram: pages 66–69. Changing lines: pages 90–97.*

# 50 DING (TING)

## THE CAULDRON, THE SACRED VESSEL

*Attributes: Transformation, nourishment, sacrifice, consecration*

This hexagram comprises Fire over Wind. Wind is connected to the element Wood, so the combination suggests flames blazing over a well-ventilated pile of firewood. This is connected to cooking, since the shape of the hexagram resembles that of a traditional Chinese *ding*, a bronze cauldron decorated with sacred inscriptions. The yang lines correspond to the body of the vessel and its lid, and the yin lines represent its two handles and two legs.

While the image of a cheerfully steaming cauldron of food has the obvious symbol of nourishment and plenty, it also exemplifies the notion of transformation. Cooking may be considered a branch of alchemy, raw ingredients being transformed into a more complex and attractive combination.

As well as containing human nourishment, the ding was also used to contain offerings of food for honoring departed ancestors and higher spiritual powers. In this context, the humble cooking pot is itself transformed into a ceremonial vessel, containing offered food just as the cauldrons of our minds offer gratitude to the higher realm.

Ding therefore represents the meeting of the physical and metaphysical dimensions, reminding us that both aspects must be attended to and respected if our lives are to be lived well.

| Line no. | Brief reading for changing line | Level of auspiciousness |
|---|---|---|
| Line 6 | Having succeeded, you must retain humility and kindness. | ★★★ This is an indication of a great omen. |
| Line 5 | Delegate responsibility wisely rather than insisting on total control. | ★ This is a sign of good fortune. |
| Line 4 | When overwhelmed with responsibility, do not share it with those unworthy of trust. | ✚✚ You may have bad luck. |
| Line 3 | Your virtues will remain unrecognized until you are engaged in an honorable task. | ★ This is a sign of good fortune. |
| Line 2 | Do not allow envy to distract you from your true purpose. | ★★ This is a sign of a good omen. |
| Line 1 | When purged of impurities, all may prove of equal worth. | ▲ There is nothing to blame. |

Overall level of auspiciousness: ★★★ This is an indication of a great omen.

*Fire trigram: pages 66–69. Wind trigram: pages 58–61. Changing lines: pages 90–97.*

# 51 ZHEN (CHEN)
## THE AROUSING, TEST TO EQUANIMITY

*Attributes: Shock, surprise, response to provocation, taking action, challenges to structure*

This hexagram comprises Thunder over Thunder, the doubling of an explosive sound provoking feelings of fear and alarm. Zhen suggests a range of events all as startling as a sudden deafening clap of thunder. These range from natural disasters to loss of wealth, humiliation, gossip, arguments, and even violence.

Such disturbing events can, however, turn out to be constructive if we are able to rise to the challenges imposed. Often, it takes a fright or catastrophe to jolt us into questioning the bases of our lives. This is reinforced by the I Ching's association of thunder with the energy of springtime.

Accordingly, by causing us to pause and consider the dangers we have inadvertently invited into our lives, the shock of Zhen often heralds a new beginning and deepening self-awareness. Much can be achieved if we take responsibility for our troubles and look for new perspectives.

Once this period of adversity and alarm has passed, there is every chance that we will find our lives to be in a healthier state. At such times we must be on guard against falling back into old patterns of thinking. Like Zhen's thunder, our power can be doubled if we seize this opportunity to learn.

| Line no. | Brief reading for changing line | Level of auspiciousness |
| --- | --- | --- |
| Line 6 | You must strive to remain calm and centered in the face of adversity. | ▲ There is nothing to blame. |
| Line 5 | A still point may be found in the midst of constant threat. | ★ This is a sign of good fortune. |
| Line 4 | This is a poor time to freeze in the face of danger. | ✚✚ You may have bad luck. |
| Line 3 | Keep mentally alert amid chaos and the worst can be avoided. | ✚ Regret will disappear. |
| Line 2 | Loss is inevitable, but only temporary. | ▲ There is nothing to blame. |
| Line 1 | A troubling situation may help to bring out the best qualities in you. | ★ This is a sign of good fortune. |

Overall level of auspiciousness: ★ This is a sign of good fortune.

*Thunder trigram: pages 54–57. Changing lines: pages 90–97.*

# 52 GEN (KEN)
## KEEPING STILL, RESTING
*Attributes: Quietude, inner peace, restraint, meditation*

This hexagram comprises Mountain over Mountain. This doubling of the stillness related to the Mountain trigram makes Gen the I Ching's primary image of calmness. As mountains are traditionally seen as places of retreat and meditation, the hexagram counsels us to withdraw from the marketplace and cultivate the inner peace necessary for further development.

While Gen advises rest from worldly activities, the meditative state it calls for is not necessarily easy for us. Achieving a tranquil heart is extremely difficult and calls for great persistence and self-discipline. True meditation requires inner as well as outer stillness, which can only be achieved through the patient, persistent quieting of our anxieties and internal chatter.

As serenity increases, we are able to perceive the world more clearly and objectively, our eyes unclouded by self-delusion and overly judgmental attitudes.

The philosophy of the I Ching does not see such stillness as our ultimate goal. Like all of the conditions of life described by the hexagrams, Gen is seen as simply one transitory state among many. However, it is through Gen's stillness that we may acquire the wisdom and nourishment of the spirit that we require in order to pass safely and calmly through all circumstances.

| Line no. | Brief reading for changing line | Level of auspiciousness |
|----------|--------------------------------|--------------------------|
| Line 6 | You have attained a level of purest tranquillity. | ★★ This is a sign of good fortune. |
| Line 5 | Guard against careless talk and your words will carry greater weight. | ▲ There is nothing to blame. |
| Line 4 | Doubt and agitation are slowly being replaced by serenity. | ▲ There is nothing to blame. |
| Line 3 | Inner calmness must be coaxed, not forced. | ✚ Regret will disappear. |
| Line 2 | Resist being led forward by unworthy desires. | ✚ Regret will disappear. |
| Line 1 | Achieve a sense of inner stillness and contemplation before action. | ★★ This is a sign of good fortune. |

Overall level of auspiciousness: ▲ There is nothing to blame.
*Mountain trigram: pages 70–73. Changing lines: pages 90–97.*

# 53 JIAN (CHIEN)
## GRADUAL PROGRESS, DEVELOPMENT
*Attributes: Steady growth, maturation, patience, lasting results, lifelong growth*

This hexagram comprises Wind over Mountain. As the Wind trigram also relates to the element Wood, Jian suggests an image of trees growing on the top of a windswept peak. In order to withstand their exposure to the elements, the trees must remain strong, well proportioned, and firmly rooted. This type of stability can only be achieved through slow and steady progress, which is also how lasting changes are achieved in human affairs.

The I Ching uses the preparation of a young couple for marriage as an example of this type of measured progress. The attendant formalities may advance slowly, but if they encourage the development of the cooperation necessary for all complex relationships, the time may be considered well spent.

The same principles apply whenever we wish to influence others. If time is not spent on nurturing new relationships and attitudes, the winds of change will uproot them just as a sapling grown too high for its girth will be brought down by the high winds of the mountaintop.

Jian warns that rapid progress and forceful behavior will complicate your present difficulties, whereas steady, considered persistence will achieve great things. If this advice is heeded, both business and relationships are well favored at this time.

| Line no. | Brief reading for changing line | Level of auspiciousness |
|---|---|---|
| Line 6 | An admirably lived life is an inspiration to all. | ★★ This is a sign of a good omen. |
| Line 5 | Someone who has long misjudged you is soon to discover this error. | ★★ This is a sign of a good omen. |
| Line 4 | You find yourself in an unsuitable situation but adapt to it. | ▲ There is nothing to blame. |
| Line 3 | In an unfavorable situation, you should defend but not attack. | ✚ Regret will disappear. |
| Line 2 | Security and good fortune should be shared. | ★★ This is a sign of a good omen. |
| Line 1 | Gradual success is achieved through caution and diligence. | ★ This is a sign of good fortune. |

Overall level of auspiciousness: ★ This is a sign of good fortune.

*Wind trigram: pages 58–61. Mountain trigram: pages 70–73. Changing lines: pages 90–97.*

# 54 GUI MEI (KUEI MEI)
## THE MARRYING MAIDEN, INEXPERIENCE

*Attributes: Disappointment, lack of substance, subordination, perspective*

This hexagram comprises Thunder over Lake. Despite the insurmountable distance between them, the water ripples beneath the rumbling of an autumnal storm. This suggests the tendency of the inexperienced (the Lake trigram is also known as "the Youngest Daughter") to easily become infatuated with individuals with whom they have little genuine connection.

The I Ching elaborates on this image, describing a young lady who has impulsively entered into a marriage, the realities of which fail to live up to her hopes. In the absence of genuine love, the basis of true union, she finds herself in a subordinate role and somewhat taken for granted.

In these situations, such mistakes must be acknowledged and tactful steps taken to remedy matters. Rushing to escape invites a painful failure. We must not compound one impetuous error with another.

Gui Mei reminds us that misunderstandings and errors in judgment may occur in all sorts of relationships, particularly where we allow ourselves to float through life ruled by whims rather than purpose. The sense of flow advocated by the I Ching is to move in accordance with the inner current of life, not to drift haphazardly under the influence of others.

| Line no. | Brief reading for changing line | Level of auspiciousness |
|---|---|---|
| Line 6 | Lip service and insincere gestures will bring no good. | ✚ Regret will disappear. |
| Line 5 | Riches are seen to be of far less worth than an honorable heart. | ★★ This is a sign of a good omen. |
| Line 4 | Some time may elapse before your reward manifests. | ✚✚ You may have bad luck. |
| Line 3 | Aspects of your hopes will be granted in ways you haven't foreseen. | ▲ There is nothing to blame. |
| Line 2 | Matters may not turn out as planned, but all is not lost. | ★★ This is a sign of a good omen. |
| Line 1 | You may need to lower your sights, but success will still come. | ★★ This is a sign of a good omen. |

Overall level of auspiciousness: ✚✚ You may have bad luck.

*Thunder trigram: pages 54–57. Lake trigram: pages 74–77. Changing lines: pages 90–97.*

# 55 FENG

## ABUNDANCE, OPPORTUNITY

*Attributes: Major achievements, effectiveness, peaking energy, bounty*

This hexagram comprises Thunder over Fire, which suggests the flashing lightning reaching earthward during a thunderstorm, a symbol of tremendous power in action. As such, Feng represents a time of supreme achievement, abundance, and success.

Since this is a peaking of our energy, it will not be long lasting, and a decrease of power must inevitably follow. We are currently like the sun at midday, but the sun will eventually set once more. There is no cause for regret in this, but we must take the fullest possible advantage of this prevailing climate of triumph to set in place the schemes and structures that will further our aims once the situation alters.

Feng counsels against excess and complacency in the face of our triumph. Like a wise leader who, having risen to power, establishes justice and order, we should not waste opportunities by indulging in self-congratulation. Careful management is called for in all matters despite the jubilant distractions around us.

At the same time, we must not let our sense of responsibility rob us of our pleasure in this particularly favorable period of our lives. We owe it to our supporters and loved ones to participate in the celebrations.

| Line no. | Brief reading for changing line | Level of auspiciousness |
|---|---|---|
| Line 6 | Selfishness can result only in isolation and a mockery of success. | ✚✚ You may have bad luck. |
| Line 5 | Your position may be greatly improved if you heed the advice of those you trust. | ★★ This is a sign of a good omen. |
| Line 4 | Your growing wisdom and insight dictate the next phase of action. | ★★ This is a sign of a good omen. |
| Line 3 | Events conspire to make action inadvisable. | ▲ There is nothing to blame. |
| Line 2 | In an atmosphere of suspicion and jealousy, patience is the wisest course. | ★★ This is a sign of a good omen. |
| Line 1 | A noncompetitive partnership will benefit both parties. | ▲ There is nothing to blame. |

Overall level of auspiciousness: ★ This is a sign of good fortune.

*Thunder trigram: pages 54–57. Fire trigram: pages 66–69. Changing lines: pages 90–97.*

# 56 LU

## THE WANDERER, TRANSITION

*Attributes: Impermanence, travel, movement, separation, quests, strangers*

This hexagram comprises Fire over Mountain, which suggests a wildfire burning through the foliage at the top of a mountain. The blaze rapidly consumes all the fuel the peak has and it must then travel in search of more. The relationship between the two trigrams embodies transience.

This image in turn represents the need that at times drives us to keep on the move, in search of something we are unable to find at home. Lu is therefore the hexagram of the seeker.

Restlessness often results from our need to find a new form of fuel in our lives, but to travel well we must be aware of its hazards. Separated from familiar securities, we must adapt to unfamiliar places and customs with caution and respect, and to strangers with courtesy, discretion, and deference. By avoiding airs and pretension, we protect ourselves against humiliation.

While traveling prevents stagnation, we must be mindful of the fact that when constantly moving we may decrease our ability to have a permanent influence on the world. Such achievements often require risks that are better made from a place of strength and stability. We must also recognize when we are traveling to escape something, rather than to seek something.

| Line no. | Brief reading for changing line | Level of auspiciousness |
|---|---|---|
| Line 6 | If you treat the troubles of others lightly, this may come back to haunt you. | ✚✚ You may have bad luck. |
| Line 5 | You may need to find some method of swaying those whose favor you seek. | ✚✚ You may have bad luck. |
| Line 4 | The insecurity of your situation begins to weary you. | ✚ Regret will disappear. |
| Line 3 | A meddling and cavalier attitude may alienate the few who currently support you. | ✚✚✚ Be very cautious—this is a warning. |
| Line 2 | A quiet, sober attitude will win you a valuable friend. | ★★ This is a sign of a good omen. |
| Line 1 | Abusing the values of others can only lead you to misfortune. | ✚ Regret will disappear. |

Overall level of auspiciousness: ★★ This is a sign of a good omen.

*Fire trigram: pages 66–69. Mountain trigram: pages 70–73. Changing lines: pages 90–97.*

# 57 XUN (SUN)

## THE PENETRATING, THE GENTLE

*Attributes: Persistence, patience, repetition, pervasiveness, proceeding with humility*

This hexagram comprises Wind over Wind. Unobtrusive and gentle, the breeze may gradually achieve great things through persistence. If the wind continually changes, it may have little effect, but when it applies its influence consistently from a single direction it will in time be proven as a force to reckon with.

In human affairs, aggressive and violent ambition often make dramatic changes, but also strengthen opposition. If we wish to effect abiding change, we are well advised to emulate the wind's gentle but unceasing labor. Intimidation is a far less effective method of persuasion than engendering trust through integrity, constancy, and humility.

The wind adapts itself to the shapes and natures of the obstacles it encounters without interrupting its subtle insistence. Similarly, a flexible nature will win us friends in our endeavors. Balance is needed, however. Excessive compliance will undermine our self-confidence and respect from others. Advancement is not possible from a crouching position.

Xun advises us that the way to lasting support for our ideas lies in patient repetition and explanation. We cannot expect endorsement of our goals unless they have permeated the hearts and minds of others, nor instructions to be carried out if they are not clearly understood.

| Line no. | Brief reading for changing line | Level of auspiciousness |
|---|---|---|
| Line 6 | You must resist the temptation to rest while dangers still lurk. | ✚ Regret will disappear. |
| Line 5 | Careful thought must be given to a matter both before and after it is arranged. | ★ This is a sign of good fortune. |
| Line 4 | Your enterprises must satisfy all your needs: spiritual, social, and personal. | ▲ There is nothing to blame. |
| Line 3 | While forethought is necessary, failure threatens if action is delayed. | ✚ Regret will disappear. |
| Line 2 | Insight is required to prevent underhanded opposition from succeeding. | ▲ There is nothing to blame. |
| Line 1 | Soldierly self-discipline will help to overcome indecision. | ★ This is a sign of good fortune. |

Overall level of auspiciousness: ★ This is a sign of good fortune.

*Wind trigram: pages 58–61. Changing lines: pages 90–97.*

# 58 DUI

## JOY, PLEASURE

*Attributes: Bliss, shared happiness, communication, openness, banishment of anxiety*

This hexagram comprises Lake over Lake, suggesting a higher lake sharing its waters with a lower one, thereby lessening its likelihood of being depleted by evaporation. Similarly, joy, knowledge, and wisdom are enhanced when shared throughout the community.

The Lake trigram symbolizes the joy that arises from a sense of stability (the two lower yang lines depict this internal strength and the upper yin line the external mildness). This trigram's influence, doubled in Dui, embodies a mood of infectious elation where beauty and celebration reign as nature offers up her harvest.

With its usual sense of the importance of balance, the I Ching reminds us not to allow this exuberance to slip into uncontrolled revelry, nor to allow the trigram's association with speech to become, through its doubling, excessive, gossipy, or quarrelsome as conversations at gatherings often do. The emphasis on speech should instead be an indication of shared goodwill, good humor, and wisdom. It may also suggest a career involving public speaking.

Dui reminds us that all we undertake in life provides an opportunity to learn and thereafter the chance to share the fruits of our endeavors. As such, each task we undertake should be embraced with pleasure.

| Line no. | Brief reading for changing line | Level of auspiciousness |
|----------|--------------------------------|-------------------------|
| Line 6 | Success has been won, but be on guard against self-indulgence. | ★ This is a sign of good fortune. |
| Line 5 | Misplaced trust threatens to undermine your achievements. | ✚ Regret will disappear. |
| Line 4 | Adjusting your values in accordance with your spiritual nature brings peace. | ★ This is a sign of good fortune. |
| Line 3 | Luxuriating in pleasant diversions will cause you to lose ground. | ✚✚ You may have bad luck. |
| Line 2 | Your personal integrity guards against intemperance. | ★★ This is a sign of a good omen. |
| Line 1 | You have reached a place of true satisfaction. | ★★ This is a sign of a good omen. |

Overall level of auspiciousness: ★★ This is a sign of a good omen.

*Lake trigram: pages 74–77. Changing lines: pages 90–97.*

# 59 HUAN
## DISPERSION, DISSOLUTION
*Attributes: Dissolving blockages, resolving conflicts, restoring unity*

This hexagram comprises Wind over Water. The two forces are not integrated, which suggests an element of disunity, but although the wind cannot penetrate the water, its effects can be seen in the ripples and waves on the water's surface.

In this way, it assists in the removal or surmounting of blockages caused by fallen branches or leaves. Likewise, a strong breeze can give water greater mobility by carrying it as spray or mist, and a warm wind in early spring will help to dissolve and disperse the ice that robs water of motion.

Communities and individuals also experience stagnation, stalemates, and rigidity of thoughts. Huan represents the need for the dispersal of such obstacles to progress, acknowledging that this sometimes entails a period of chaos. In order to break through major obstructions, the wind must often whip up powerful waves. Once unleashed, they may become a fearsome force of destruction, and Huan warns us against becoming lost in the confusion.

Wind and the element Wood are related in the I Ching. Through the image of Wood on Water, Huan also suggests the boats, which allow separated individuals to reunite. In divination it may suggest a new venture, travel, or a change of home or career.

| Line no. | Brief reading for changing line | Level of auspiciousness |
|----------|--------------------------------|-------------------------|
| Line 6 | Take steps to prevent harm from befalling you and those you love. | ▲ There is nothing to blame. |
| Line 5 | In the midst of a crisis, a solution suddenly reveals itself. | ▲ There is nothing to blame. |
| Line 4 | Personal matters are put aside in order to achieve mutual benefit. | ★★★ This is an indication of a great omen. |
| Line 3 | The current task requires you to put the work before your self-interests. | ▲ There is nothing to blame. |
| Line 2 | Your inner calmness and detachment will carry you through your troubles. | ▲ There is nothing to blame. |
| Line 1 | Misunderstandings must be corrected as soon as they are observed. | ★★ This is a sign of a good omen. |

Overall level of auspiciousness: ★ This is a sign of good fortune.

*Wind trigram: pages 58–61. Water trigram: pages 62–65. Changing lines: pages 90–97.*

# 60 JIE (CHIEH)
## LIMITATION, MODERATION
*Attributes: Self-restraint, necessary restrictions, discipline, equilibrium*

This hexagram comprises Water over Lake, which suggests rain falling into the lake. If there is insufficient rain, the lake will dry up; if there is too much, it may cause devastation through overflowing. Jie is, therefore, the hexagram of moderation and the application of sensible limits.

Just as there exists vastly more water in our world than a single lake could hold, so the riches and complexities of life are infinite while we are finite vessels. If a lake received unlimited amounts of water it would no longer be a lake, and if we attempt to absorb more from life than we are constitutionally able to bear, we would likewise lose our identity. Knowledge of our limitations allows us to prevent the dangers of overindulgence.

It is easy to see that self-restraint prepares us for hardships and that thrift today assures us of opportunity tomorrow. However, we must be careful not to allow moderation to turn into asceticism. To limit ourselves and others too harshly is to allow the lake to be reduced to mud. Severe regulation leads to oppression, rebellion, and declining prosperity.

Jie reminds us that even limitations have their limits and we must each find our "middle ground" throughout our lives.

| Line no. | Brief reading for changing line | Level of auspiciousness |
|---|---|---|
| Line 6 | Attempting to enforce overly strict rules will cause problems. | ✚ Regret will disappear. |
| Line 5 | Working together with shared aims and responsibilities will succeed. | ★★ This is a sign of a good omen. |
| Line 4 | Working within your acknowledged limits is the correct course. | ★★ This is a sign of a good omen. |
| Line 3 | Extravagance and self-indulgence will solve nothing. | ▲ There is nothing to blame. |
| Line 2 | Trouble will arise unless you seize the right moment to act. | ✚ Regret will disappear. |
| Line 1 | Trust yourself to know when to act and when to be patient. | ▲ There is nothing to blame. |

Overall level of auspiciousness: ★ This is a sign of good fortune.

*Water trigram: pages 62–65. Lake trigram: pages 74–77. Changing lines: pages 90–97.*

# 61 ZHONG FU (CHUNG FU)
## INNER TRUTH, SINCERITY
*Attributes: Compassion, willingness to grow, spiritual development, transformation*

This hexagram comprises Wind over Lake, suggesting the dancing of ripples on the lake's surface as a gentle breeze plays over it. As the invisible is made visible by the ripples, so may the realm of spiritual existence be perceived through the actions of those it touches.

The shape of the hexagram suggests both an open heart (the small space created by the central yin lines in the otherwise solid form) and the meeting of lips in a kiss (the trigrams mirroring each other). Both images reinforce Zhong Fu's recommendation that we devote our efforts to becoming more receptive to universal compassion and the spiritual truths that transcend individual and cultural differences.

Gentleness and understanding create more willingness in others to follow than force or intimidation can, but their effectiveness requires the utmost sincerity and a refusal to pander to the whims of ego. When mutual trust is undermined by self-interest, far-reaching and permanent progress is impossible. Few forces are more destructive to prosperity than the resentment bred by misplaced trust and affection.

As long as the atmosphere associated with Zhong Fu is free from dishonesty and prejudice, this is an exceptionally auspicious time for all enterprises of communal benefit.

| Line no. | Brief reading for changing line | Level of auspiciousness |
|---|---|---|
| Line 6 | Mere words may inspire action but do not achieve results by themselves. | ✚ Regret will disappear. |
| Line 5 | You need to become the focal point for a group project. | ▲ There is nothing to blame. |
| Line 4 | Progress is possible when the group is bound by mutual trust. | ▲ There is nothing to blame. |
| Line 3 | Inner calm is necessary to counterbalance the emotional flux of social life. | ✚ Regret will disappear. |
| Line 2 | It will benefit you to seek the company of kindred spirits. | ★★ This is a sign of a good omen. |
| Line 1 | A sense of tranquillity is possible in the absence of relentless scheming. | ★★ This is a sign of a good omen. |

Overall level of auspiciousness: ★ This is a sign of good fortune.

*Wind trigram: pages 58–61. Lake trigram: pages 74–77. Changing lines: pages 90–97.*

# 62 XIAO GUO (HSAIO KUO)
## THE PREPONDERANCE OF THE SMALL, HUMILITY
*Attributes: Attending to details, minute adjustments, modesty, adapting to circumstances*

This hexagram comprises Thunder over Mountain. While the mountaintop may seem very close to the source of thunder, the earthbound stillness of the peak does not allow it to rise any closer. As the thunder's echoes gradually diminish, it is as if they remind the mountain to attend to mundane matters rather than the exalted.

The form of the hexagram also suggests the form of a bird with its wings raised for flight, but Xiao Guo advises the bird that while the thunder rages this is not the time for ambitious flight. It is wiser to fly down the mountain to the safety of the nest. The hexagram likewise informs us that this is a time for attending to humble duties rather than grandiose plans.

In this climate, we will find it difficult to make any significant advancement, and opportunities may be lost despite our hard work. Our best course is to maintain a low profile and concentrate on small challenges until we have a clearer picture of how to proceed.

In doing so, however, we must not altogether abandon ambition and purpose. The self-negation of excessive humility may spread to meanness and disrespectfulness toward others.

| Line no. | Brief reading for changing line | Level of auspiciousness |
|---|---|---|
| Line 6 | Nothing can be gained from pushing beyond the limits of safety. | ✚✚ You may have bad luck. |
| Line 5 | Despite unpromising appearances, success may still be achieved. | ✚ Regret will disappear. |
| Line 4 | Inward alertness and outward calm are required. | ▲ There is nothing to blame. |
| Line 3 | Danger approaches from an unexpected source. | ✚✚ You may have bad luck. |
| Line 2 | Self-restraint and modesty in social interactions are called for. | ▲ There is nothing to blame. |
| Line 1 | Your sense of adventure may lead to disaster. | ✚✚ You may have bad luck. |

Overall level of auspiciousness: ★ This is a sign of good fortune.

*Thunder trigram: pages 54–57. Mountain trigram: pages 70–73. Changing lines: pages 90–97.*

# 63 JI JI (CHI CHI)
## AFTER COMPLETION, THE RIVER CROSSED
*Attributes: Fulfillment, well-earned success, final details, consolidation*

This hexagram comprises Water over Fire, which suggests a kettle suspended over a fire. Unlike hexagram 64 (where the trigrams are reversed), here the two combine to produce a desired effect. The harmony of the yin and yang lines' alternation further emphasizes a correct arrangement of resources.

While Ji Ji symbolizes victory, it reminds us that vigilance is still needed to see that our gains are firmly established. If the water in the kettle is untended, it may boil over and extinguish the fire; if the fire is neglected, it may produce too much heat and boil the kettle empty. Balance and harmony are always fragile.

In all aspects of life the I Ching warns against complacency, and at the successful conclusion of a long undertaking, we are more than usually prone to this failing. Ji Ji emphasizes that a period of consolidation is necessary if our project is to enjoy continued success. In this moment of release from anxiety, we must not indulge too heavily in celebration. Our focus must be on perfecting the situation and guarding against reversals.

We are also advised not to embark on another ambitious enterprise immediately. Our initial elation could soon turn to exhaustion and schemes well started could end poorly.

| Line no. | Brief reading for changing line | Level of auspiciousness |
|---|---|---|
| Line 6 | Having escaped a place of danger, it would be foolhardy to return there. | ✚✚✚ Be very cautious—this is a warning. |
| Line 5 | Sincerity triumphs over ostentation. | ★ This is a sign of good fortune. |
| Line 4 | Remain aware that all things, triumphs as much as failures, must pass. | ✚ Regret will disappear. |
| Line 3 | Having achieved progress, do not let misplaced trust tarnish the triumph. | ✚ Regret will disappear. |
| Line 2 | Press on rather than pausing to try to reverse small losses. | ▲ There is nothing to blame. |
| Line 1 | An impulsive beginning needs to be slowed down judiciously. | ▲ There is nothing to blame. |

Overall level of auspiciousness: ★ This is a sign of good fortune.

*Water trigram: pages 62–65. Fire trigram: pages 66–69. Changing lines: pages 90–97.*

# 64 WEI JI (WEI CHI)
## BEFORE COMPLETION, THE RIVER NOT YET CROSSED
*Attributes: Incomplete fulfillment, continued effort, transition, preparation for action, approaching success*

This hexagram comprises Fire over Water. While the shape of the hexagram (two opposite trigrams and a regular alternation of yin and yang lines) suggests order, the upwardly rising fire and downwardly flowing water have no effect on each other. The opposite of hexagram 63, this shows an enterprise nearing completion but still requiring diligent work.

At such times we may be in danger of ruining our work by rushing toward the end without attending to unfinished details or resolving possible misunderstandings. Either frustration or bravado could prove our undoing and should be guarded against.

The I Ching offers an image for this of a young fox attempting to cross the thin ice of a frozen stream. In his haste to reach dry land he is careless in his final leap and allows his tail to splash into the cold water. We must be careful not to fall into the same error and have a probable victory reduced to an embarrassing failure.

The period of transition as we near the end of a project is a dangerous time but Wei Ji suggests that with deliberation, patience, and caution, success is well within our grasp.

| Line no. | Brief reading for changing line | Level of auspiciousness |
|---|---|---|
| Line 6 | Enjoy the expectation of coming success without falling prey to overindulgence. | ▲ There is nothing to blame. |
| Line 5 | A major success has been achieved, for which you are greatly admired. | ★★ This is a sign of a good omen. |
| Line 4 | A final push against your opposition is necessary before victory is yours. | ★★ This is a sign of a good omen. |
| Line 3 | Do not attempt to fight your opposition on their choice of battlefield. | ✚ Regret will disappear. |
| Line 2 | Although success is within your grasp, a period of waiting is required. | ★★ This is a sign of a good omen. |
| Line 1 | Be wary of allowing success to slip away by acting impulsively. | ▲ There is nothing to blame. |

Overall level of auspiciousness: ▲ There is nothing to blame.

*Fire trigram: pages 66–69. Water trigram: pages 62–65. Changing lines: pages 90–97.*

# YOUR REFLECTIONS ON THE I CHING

As you have found when casting and reading the hexagrams, the I Ching can bring much wisdom into your life. The list below offers a wise saying relating to each hexagram, numbered accordingly. Take time to think about and meditate upon each of these.

You can also look back at the explanation of the hexagram in this chapter and reflect upon what the saying can contribute to your understanding of your own life and where you are going. Write your thoughts in your I Ching journal and come back to them whenever you consult the I Ching with a new question.

1. "You must be persistent and steadfast in virtuous ways."
2. "You must not only be submissive and responsive to heaven's will, but you must also remain true to yourself."
3. "You must be patient through the time of a difficult birth."
4. "The student must seek a wise teacher and be sincere in the quest to learn."
5. "Patiently cooperate with time. Living in the joyous expectation of the best attracts the best to you."
6. "Mistrusting the nature of things will assuredly lead us from one conflict to the next. Cultivate faith in harmony."
7. "Without discipline, true leadership cannot exist. But this discipline should not be forced. To embrace the people is to nurture the five virtues: benevolence, justice, courtesy, wisdom and knowledge, and truthfulness."
8. "Where there is mutual trust and support, undertakings will be successful."
9. "Before we can progress, we are often required to take a temporary break in which to gather energy."
10. "Allow your path to be guided by courtesy and composure."
11. "Good fortune arises from achieving a balanced attitude and alignment with the higher powers of life."
12. "As we reach the depths of misfortune, matters begin to change to their opposites."

13. "Cooperation, mutual respect, and shared values can only strengthen us."
14. "By remaining modest and generous we allow abundance to express itself in graceful and controlled ways."
15. "Humility is the way to develop your spirit endlessly."
16. "We must value the sacred ceremonies that bring relief and motivation through joy, hope, and celebration."
17. "We must learn the ways of leadership and service equally well."
18. "We must confront the problems of our past before true progress is possible."
19. "We progress securely when we recognize and take advantage of optimal times for growth."
20. "We must remain ever watchful while recognizing ourselves as part of the wholeness."
21. "Harmony is furthered when human law governs justly."
22. "Your good fortune will be increased at this time if you concentrate on bringing more grace into your thoughts and actions."
23. "When matters have reached their worst, they will inevitably begin to improve."
24. "The cycle of existence moves steadily toward a better future and so we need not push matters at this time."
25. "We benefit from aligning our attitudes and motivations with the natural unfolding of life."
26. "Preparation and the gathering of resources will lead to an increase of wealth and a broadening of horizons."
27. "We must strive to exercise discretion and wisdom in every meal and every word that passes our lips."
28. "As pressure mounts, we must act before disaster can strike."
29. "Confronted correctly, danger can help us reinforce our inner strength."
30. "Enlightenment requires us to allow the truth to shine into the deepest part of our being."
31. "Good fortune follows when natural affinity is enriched by mutual support."
32. "Where there is sincerity and generosity, union and success will endure."
33. "At times retreat may prove wiser and worthier than confrontation."

34. "As we become stronger, it is essential to remember that true greatness depends upon being in harmony with what is right."
35. "Genuine progress may be determined by how far we have distanced ourselves from inferior influences."
36. "In times of darkness, we must often learn to conceal our light in order to preserve it."
37. "Like the happiest of families, we must try to unite in mutual affection, respect, and inspiration."
38. "Great opportunity arises when opposites are reconciled."
39. "When danger threatens without, we should find stillness and stability within."
40. "When moving away from danger, we travel fastest when unburdened by resentment."
41. "When we are unattached to material wealth and can share openheartedly, good fortune prevails."
42. "When worldly advancement and internal betterment act together, their potency is doubled."
43. "By anticipating and preparing for confrontation, we are able to deal with it on our own terms."
44. "Vigilance is necessary to perceive encroaching negative influences before they gain strength."
45. "Communities achieve prosperity by acting in accord."
46. "When the time is ripe for expansion, progress is best achieved through patient, unforced persistence."
47. "The most extreme misfortune may bestow seeds of regeneration to those with the strength to seek them."
48. "The spirit must be nourished from a source that lies beneath the surface of life."
49. "Innovation and radical change are possible once we are prepared to rid ourselves of doubt and fear."
50. "Our lives are in balance when both their inner and outer aspects are well ordered."
51. "The laughter of relief often follows on the heels of a cry of alarm."
52. "Through self-discipline and stillness, we may attain mastery of the mind and body."

53. "Among the most essential ingredients of mutual understanding, harmonious relationships, and enduring change are time and patience."
54. "By remaining aware that our current lives are finite, we may be better served by applying ourselves to attaining real achievement."
55. "A wise person knows how to take full advantage of prosperity."
56. "To see the world clearly we may sometimes need to be a stranger to it."
57. "Proceeding with gentle persistence is the most effective way to influence events."
58. "Satisfaction and joy inspire us to greater efforts."
59. "We must sometimes summon crashing waves to erode barriers to unity."
60. "Moderation is wise in all things, including moderation."
61. "The greatest strength is derived from trust and compassion."
62. "By applying ourselves to small matters, we create the foundation of future success."
63. "Even after victory, equilibrium requires maintenance."
64. "Overconfidence and inattention may bring the surest triumph to disaster."

## CHAPTER SEVEN

# OUR INTERACTION WITH THE SPIRITUAL

*How to develop your skills further. Discover your ming gua number.*

The I Ching is a book of divination, giving us insight into what the present offers and what the future holds for us. However, in various Chinese philosophies it is believed that our fate can be strengthened if we pay heed to our ming gua number and associated directions.

The *ming gua* is a form of what is commonly called Chinese astrology. All forms of Chinese astrology should more properly be known as divination, because they examine the relationships over time of the five elements, the eight trigrams, and the balance between yin and yang rather than the movement of the constellations.

A ming gua reading involves:
• Using calculations to determine a person's ming gua number, taking into account their sex and birth date and whether they were born in the Northern or Southern Hemisphere.
• Charting their four "lucky directions," also known as *ji wei.*
• Finding the ideal orientations for the person, especially auspicious sleeping and sitting directions.

Knowing your ming gua number and directions can help determine the strength of your fate or "Heaven Luck." In ancient Chinese beliefs, there are three types of luck. Apart from Heaven Luck, there is Earth Luck and also the luck that you create for yourself, such as your virtues, thoughts, deeds, and education. Earth Luck can be calculated for a person at a given time, judging how strongly attuned a person is to the currents of energy, or qi, around them.

Heaven Luck derives from the flow of qi that was occurring during our time in the womb and when we first drew breath. The nature of the qi around us then is very influential, as we have absorbed this vibration into our bodies and souls. When we align to the same kind of energy as our natal flow of qi, things seem to run more smoothly in our lives. This is why it is important to align our bodies and our life force with these currents.

Once you have calculated your ming gua number, you will see that you belong to one of two groups: the East Life Group or the West Life Group. Each group corresponds with a particular type of energy—yin or yang—and with a particular set of compass directions and trigrams. This type of classification has been in practice for at least 2,000 years.

Once the ming gua number is calculated, you can integrate these auspicious directions into sectors of the bedroom and for desks and other sitting areas. The more we face the four directions aligned to our own personal vibrations, the better things will be for us, whether in maintaining personal relationships, career, finances, health, or our ability to study well and make sound decisions. Consider sitting facing these directions when consulting the I Ching.

## CALCULATING YOUR MING GUA NUMBER

Ming gua numbers are calculated according to a person's year of birth. This number indicates the energy, trigram, element, and other aspects that were predominant during that year for men and women. This number changes each year. As year follows year, the numbers and energies follow one another. For men, these numbers descend because the yang meridians spiral downward, and for women the numbers ascend because the yin meridians spiral upward.

Every nine years, the cycle of nine repeats. Take into account that the Chinese year begins on February 4 in the Northern Hemisphere and on August 7 in the Southern Hemisphere.

The following formulas work for all birth years from 1901 onward.

| Solar year begins | | Gender | Century number, 1900–1999 | Century number, 2000–2099 |
|---|---|---|---|---|
| **Southern** | August 7 | Male | 4 | 5 |
| **Hemisphere** | | Female | 0 | 1 |
| **Northern** | February 5 | Male | 0 | 1 |
| **Hemisphere** | | Female | 4 | 7 |

## CALCULATION

- Determine birth year (based on when the solar year begins).
- Add century number (from table above) to last two digits of year.
- Continue to add individual digits together until a single number is reached.
- For females, the result is the ming gua number.
- For males, subtract result from 10 to get the ming gua number.
- If the ming gua number is 5, assign a ming gua number of 8 for females and 2 for males to calculate lucky directions.

Note: The Northern Hemisphere year begins February 5; the Southern Hemisphere year begins August 7. Anyone born before these dates should use the date of the previous year.

### EXAMPLES FOR MALES BORN 1900–1999

*For a male born in the Southern Hemisphere, November 1970*

- 70 + 4 = 74 (solar year + century number)
- 7 + 4 = 11, 1 + 1 = 2 (add individual digits)
- 10 – 2 = 8 (subtract result from 10 to calculate male ming gua number)

*For a male born in the Southern Hemisphere, August 1, 1968*

- 67 + 4 = 71 (adjusted solar year is 1967 + century number)
- 7 + 1 = 8 (add individual digits)
- 10 – 2 = 8 (subtract result from 10 to calculate male ming gua number)

*For a male born in the Northern Hemisphere, January 1941*

- 40 + 0 = 40 (adjusted solar year is 1940 + century number)
- 4 + 0 = 4 (add individual digits)
- 10 – 4 = 6 (subtract result from 10 to calculate male ming gua number)

*For a male born in the Northern Hemisphere, December 1977*
- 77 + 0 = 77 (solar year + century number)
- 7 + 7 = 14, 1 + 4 = 5 (add individual digits)
- 10 – 5 = 5 (subtract result from 10 to calculate male ming gua number)
- 5 = 2 (if the ming gua number is 5, assign a ming gua number of 2 for males)

## EXAMPLES FOR MALES BORN 2000–2099

*For a male born in the Southern Hemisphere, November 2000*
- 00 + 5 = 5 (solar year + century number)
- 10 – 5 = 5 (subtract result from 10 to calculate male ming gua number)
- 5 = 2 (if the ming gua number is 5, assign a ming gua number of 2 for males)

*For a male born in the Southern Hemisphere, April 2011*
- 10 + 5 = 15 (adjusted solar year is 2010 + century number)
- 1 + 5 = 6 (add individual digits)
- 10 – 6 = 4 (subtract result from 10 to calculate male ming gua number)

*For a male born in the Northern Hemisphere, January 2002*
- 01 + 1 = 2 (adjusted solar year is 2001 + century number)
- 10 – 2 = 8 (subtract result from 10 to calculate male ming gua number)

*For a male born in the Northern Hemisphere, February 2011*
- 11 + 1 = 12 (solar year + century number)
- 1 + 2 = 3 (add individual digits)
- 10 – 3 = 7 (subtract result from 10 to calculate male ming gua number)

## EXAMPLES FOR FEMALES BORN 1900–1999

*For a female born in the Southern Hemisphere, June 1965*
- 64 + 0 = 64 (adjusted solar year is 1964 + century number)
- 6 + 4 = 10, 1 + 0 = 1 (add individual digits)

*For a female born in the Southern Hemisphere, August 10, 1999*
- 99 + 0 = 99 (solar year + century number)
- 9 + 9 = 18, 1 + 8 = 9 (add individual digits)

*For a female born in the Northern Hemisphere, January 1983*
- 82 + 4 = 86 (adjusted solar year is 1982 + century number)
- 6 + 4 = 10, 1 + 0 = 1 (add individual digits)

*For a female born in the Northern Hemisphere, May 1932*
- 32 + 4 = 36 (solar year + century number)
- 3 + 6 = 9 (add individual digits)

**EXAMPLES FOR FEMALES BORN 2000–2099**
*For a female born in the Southern Hemisphere, August 10, 2001*
- 01 + 1 = 2 (solar year + century number)

*For a female born in the Southern Hemisphere, January 2013*
- 12 + 1 = 13 (adjusted solar year is 2012 + century number)
- 1 + 3 = 4 (add individual digits)

*For a female born in the Northern Hemisphere, October 2000*
- 00 + 7 = 7 (solar year + century number)

*For a female born in the Northern Hemisphere, January 2013*
- 12 + 7 = 19 (adjusted solar year is 2012 + century number)
- 1 + 9= 10, 1 + 0 = 1 (add individual digits)

# HOW TO USE YOUR LUCKY MING GUA NUMBER

Once you know your ming gua number you can determine your group of lucky directions, governing element, and lucky trigram by referring to the charts on page 183 to locate your lucky directions. If you are a 5, the group you belong to is the West Life Group.

**Example: Male born in April 1958, Northern Hemisphere**
Follow the calculations on page 180. Your ming gua number is 6. Check the Northern Hemisphere chart on page 183. The number 6 corresponds to the West Life Group. If you are part of this group, face northwest, west, southwest, or northeast when sleeping or sitting at your desk.

## NORTHERN HEMISPHERE

| EAST LIFE GROUP: Yang | | | | WEST LIFE GROUP: Yin | | | |
|---|---|---|---|---|---|---|---|
| Ming gua number | Trigram name | Direction | Element | Ming gua number | Trigram name | Direction | Element |
| 1 | Water | N | Water | 2 | Earth | SW | Earth |
| 3 | Thunder | E | Wood | 8 | Mountain | NE | Earth |
| 4 | Wind | SE | Wood | 7 | Lake | W | Metal |
| 9 | Fire | S | Fire | 6 | Heaven | NW | Metal |

## SOUTHERN HEMISPHERE

| EAST LIFE GROUP: Yang | | | | WEST LIFE GROUP: Yin | | | |
|---|---|---|---|---|---|---|---|
| Ming gua number | Trigram name | Direction | Element | Ming gua number | Trigram name | Direction | Element |
| 1 | Water | S | Water | 2 | Earth | NW | Earth |
| 3 | Thunder | E | Wood | 8 | Mountain | SE | Earth |
| 4 | Wind | NE | Wood | 7 | Lake | W | Metal |
| 9 | Fire | N | Fire | 6 | Heaven | SW | Metal |

By placing your bed, desk, or favorite chair so that it faces the direction favorable to you, you will attract beneficial energy into your life. You will find that if you sit at your desk or stand at your workstation facing any of your lucky directions, you can concentrate better and will be able to enhance your good fortune. If you place your bed in a position where your head is pointing in your lucky direction, you will find that you will be able to sleep more soundly and restfully.

# FURTHER READING

Blofeld, J. *I Ching: The Book of Changes*. Mandala Books (Unwin), London, 1980 reprint.

Lawler, J. *Dragon Insights: A Simple Approach to the I Ching*. Simon & Schuster, Sydney, 2001.

Legge, J. *I Ching: Book of Changes* (trans.). Gramercy Books, New York, 1996.

Schoenholtz, L. *New Directions in the I Ching: The Yellow River Legacy*. University Books Inc., Secaucus, New Jersey, 1974.

Toropov, B. *I Ching for Beginners*. Writers and Readers Publishing Inc., New York, 1996.

Tsu, Lao. *Tao Te Ching*. Penguin, London, 1983 reprint.

Watts, A. *Tao: The Watercourse Way*. Penguin, New York, 1981 reprint.

Wilhelm, R. *I Ching or Book of Changes* (trans.). Routledge & Kegan Paul, London, 1980 reprint.

# ANSWERS TO WORKBOOK EXERCISES

**Page 21:** *Yin, yang, yin, yang, yin, yang, yin, yang*

**Page 85:** *1) Hexagram 29—Kan*

> *2) Two heads, one tail; one head, two tails; two heads, one tail; three tails; three heads; one head, two tails*

**Page 87:** *1) Two heads, one tail; three heads; two tails, one head; three tails; two tails, one head; two heads, one tail*

> *2) Yellow; blue; yellow; blue; green; green*

**Page 103:** *1) Hexagram 59—Huan*

> *2) i. Yes, ii. Yes, hexagram 28—Da Guo, from nuclear hexagram Group 1*

> *3) i. Hexagram 24—Fu, from nuclear hexagram Group 2*
>> *ii. Success as the yielding lines are supported by the lower yang line*
>> *iii. Thunder (lower), Earth (upper)*
>> *iv. Thunder is the eldest son and Earth is mother*

# GLOSSARY

**Bagua**: A configuration of eight trigrams and their corresponding numbers, which is also referred to as the "Universal Chart," representing the universe and life.

**Ben gua**: (Chinese) The original hexagram—before the **progressed hexagram** is formed (see also **hexagram**).

**Changing lines**: Also known as moving lines; represent situations where the yang or yin energy in a situation has reached its most extreme point and a change will occur, resulting in a yang line changing to a yin line or a yin line changing to a yang line. Changing lines indicate that the present situation is in a transformative stage.

**Chi**: See **Qi**.

**Dui**: The Lake trigram, also known as "the Joyous."

**Elements**: There are five elements underlying Chinese Taoist philosophy: Metal, Water, Wood, Fire, and Earth. It is believed that everything on earth, including human beings, is made up of a combination of these five elements.

**Feng shui**: The Chinese art of placement of objects in the home and the surrounding environment to stimulate the flow of beneficial energy, or qi.

**Gen**: The Mountain trigram, also known as "the Stillness," "the Stable," and "the Revolutionary."

**Gua**: (Chinese) The **trigrams**.

**Hara**: See **tantien**.

**Hexagram**: A stack of six broken and unbroken lines that indicate various fundamental spiritual principles. Each hexagram is made from two **trigrams**—three-line figures. There are three types of hexagrams—the first or original hexagram, the **progressed hexagram**, which is constructed if the first or original hexagram contains changing lines, and a **nuclear hexagram**, which is constructed of two trigrams made from the middle four lines of the first or original hexagram.

**Hu gua**: (Chinese) The **nuclear hexagram**.

**I Ching**: Translated variously as "The Book of Changes" or "The Classic of Change." Perhaps the oldest existing writing on philosophy, cosmology, divination, and self-transformation in Chinese civilization. It has been often called the philosophical backbone to traditional Chinese medicine and feng shui.

**Kan**: The Water trigram, also known as "the Cautious," "the Depth," "the Dangerous," or "the Abysmal."

**Kun**: The Earth trigram, also known as "the Responding."

**Lao Tsu**: (604–531 B.C.) A great sage who wrote the *Tao Te Ching*.

**Li**: The Fire trigram, also known as "the Clinging."

**Locked hexagram**: Occurs when a hexagram does not contain any changing lines. This means that the answer to a question is very definite and specific and the situation you are dealing with is fixed.

**Nuclear hexagram**: Also known as *hu gua*, this type of hexagram is constructed out of two nuclear trigrams "hidden" within the original hexagram. This hexagram indicates the secret meaning or origins of the situation. All nuclear hexagrams eventually reduce down to four groups of hexagrams, grouped under hexagram 1 (Qian), hexagram 2 (Kun), hexagram 63 (Ji Ji), and hexagram 64 (Wei Ji).

**Plastromancy**: Using the cracks in the shells of tortoises, which are symbolic of wisdom gathered over a long life, to foretell the future.

**Progressed hexagram**: Also known as *zhi gua*, this is the hexagram that comprises the unchanged lines of the original hexagram (*ben gua*) and the lines that have been changed from yin to yang or from yang to yin.

**Qi**: (also known as *chi* or *ki*) An invisible but powerful energy that flows around and within everything in the universe. It is created and stimulated by the balance of two extreme forms of energy that are known as yang (male) and yin (female). There are many levels of qi, such as heaven qi, earth qi, and human qi. There are also more intimate levels of qi, such as personal qi, which reflects the energy that moves through your body, thoughts, emotions, and personality. Every organ in your body has its particular quality of qi; for example, there is a kidney qi, a heart qi, and a liver qi.

**Qian**: The Heaven trigram, also known as "the Creative" or "the Initiating."

**San cai**: (Chinese) Refers to the three treasures or the Taoist trinity of heaven, earth, and humanity. The upper line of the trigram represents heaven while the bottom line symbolizes earth. Humanity is represented as the middle line. This is also known as the trinity principle of cosmic unity.

**Synchronicity**: A word coined by Carl Jung from his study of the I Ching, which refers to situations when seemingly related things happen simultaneously for no apparent related cause.

**Tantien**: (Chinese) Also known as **hara** in Japanese, this is our own energy center, through which we can contact our higher self.

**Tao**: Taoism, along with Confucianism

and Buddhism, is one of the three great philosophies of China. *Tao* can be translated as "path." The I Ching contains a wealth of Taoist knowledge, including the Taoist notions of "oneness" and that everything in the universe is part of a continuum.

**Trigrams**: There are eight trigrams, which were believed to unveil the heavenly processes in nature and to aid in the understanding of the character of everything—they could be used to depict and explain the existence of all physical, psychological, natural, and social manifestations. In a hexagram, the lower trigram indicates the cause of the situation and the upper indicates the surface appearances of the issue.

**Universal Creative Order**: The way of nature, alternating between expansion and contraction—yin and yang.

**Xun**: The Wind trigram, also known as "the Penetrating."

**Yin and yang**: These are the two great primordial forces of nature. According to Chinese Taoist philosophy, everything was created through the interaction of yin and yang. They govern the cycle of birth, growth, and decay of all things material, mental, and spiritual. Yin corresponds with female, passive energy and flexibility, and yang with male, active energy and firmness of will.

**Yang line correct**: When a yang line occurs on the first, third, or fifth line of a hexagram.

**Yin line correct**: When a yin line occurs on the second, fourth, or sixth line of a hexagram.

**Ying**: (Chinese) Meaning "resonance"; there is also a resonance, or ying, between the first and fourth, the second and fifth, and the third and sixth lines of a hexagram.

**Zhen**: The Thunder trigram, also known as "the Arousing."

**Zhi gua**: (Chinese) The progressed hexagram.

# INDEX

**A**

acupuncture, 9, 18
altar
    making, 34
    ritual at, 42
astrology, 9, 18, 178

**B**

bagua, 24
bead-casting method, 86–87
ben gua, 30
Bi hexagram, 117, 131
breathing, 37
Buddhism, 10

**C**

casting
    beads, 86–87
    coins, 81–85
    methods of, 80–81
change, 19–20
changing lines, 9, 90–95
    position and meaning, 92–95
chi exercise, 9
Chinese trinity, 17
Chou, Duke of, 9
Chou dynasty, 29
Chou Hsin, 29
clearing your mind, 34
coins, 81
    coin-casting method, 83–85
    ritual instruments, 82
    selecting, 81–82

**C**

Confucianism, 10
core hexagrams, 99
cosmic unity, 25
Cui (Tsui) hexagram, 154

**D**

Da Guo (Ta Kuo) hexagram, 137
Da Xu (Da Chui) hexagram, 135
Da You hexagram, 123
Da Zhuang (Ta Chuang) hexagram, 143
Ding (Ting) hexagram, 159
Dui hexagram, 167
Dui trigram, 75–77
Dun (Tun) hexagram, 142

**E**

Early Heaven Sequence, 24
Earth, 16, 24, 27
Earth Luck, 178
earth qi, 16
Earth trigram, 51–53, 78
East Life Group, 179
eight trigrams, 25, 27, 44–79
elements, 16–17, 24
energy
    patterns of, 10
    stimulating energy flow, 37
    universal, 16–17

**F**

Feng hexagram, 164
feng shui, 9, 18, 24, 48
Fire, 17, 24, 27

Fire trigram, 67–69
food energetics, 9
Fu hexagram, 133
Fu Xi, 9, 22–25, 27, 29

**G**
Ge (Ko) hexagram, 158
Gen (Ken) hexagram, 161
Gen trigram, 71–73
Gou (Kou) hexagram, 153
Great Ultimate, 18
gua, 22
Guai (Kuai) hexagram, 152
Guan hexagram, 129
Gu hexagram, 127
Gui Mei (Kuei Mei) hexagram, 163

**H**
Han dynasty, 24
hara, 37
heat application, 9
Heaven, 27
Heaven Luck, 178–179
heaven qi, 16
Heaven trigram, 47–49, 78
Heng hexagram, 141
herbal medicine, 9
hexagrams, 8, 28
    advanced readings, 90–103
    answer, interpreting, 106–107
    changing lines, 9, 90–95
    guide to, 108–109
    how to construct, 80–89
    identifying, 88
    interpreting, 88
    lines in, 108–109
    locked, 95
    origins, 29
    sixty-four, 29, 104–177

strategy for reading, 104–105
    three types of, 30
    using, 30
    what hexagrams tell us, 29
Huan hexagram, 168
hu gua, 30, 98–103
human qi, 16

**I**
I Ching
    aim, 11
    authorship, 9
    book of divination, 178
    building blocks, 22–24, 44
    chapters, 28
    classic book, 8
    consulting, 32–43
    honoring, 33
    key concepts, 16–31
    oracle, as, 11
    origins, 9
    reflections on, 174–177
    ritual, 42
    study of change, 19–20
    tools, safety of, 88

**J**
Jian (Chen) hexagram, 148
Jian (Chien) hexagram, 162
Jia Ren (Chia Jen) hexagram, 146
Ji wei, 178
Jie (Chieh) hexagram, 169
Jie (Hsieh) hexagram, 149
Ji Ji (Chi Chi) hexagram, 172
Jing (Chin) hexagram, 144
Jing (Ching) hexagram, 157

**K**
Kan hexagram, 138
Kan trigram, 63–65
kidney qi, 16
Kua T'uan, 29
Kui (Ku) hexagram, 147
Kun hexagram, 111, 156
Kun trigram, 51–53

**L**
Lake, 27
Lake trigram, 75–77
Later Heaven Sequence, 24
Li hexagram, 139
Lin hexagram, 128
Li trigram, 67–69
locked hexagram, 95
Lo Shu, 23
luck, 178
lucky directions, 178, 182
lucky ming gua number, 182–183
Lu hexagram, 119, 165

**M**
Magic Square, 23
meditation, 9, 35
Meng hexagram, 113
Metal, 17, 24
ming gua, 178
    lucky number, using, 182
    number, calculating, 179–182
    reading, 178
Ming Yi (Ming I) hexagram, 145
Mountain, 27
Mountain trigram, 71–73

**N**
nuclear hexagrams, 30, 98–103

numbers, 24

**P**
patterns of energy, 10
Peace hexagram, 29
personal qi, 16, 17
Pi hexagram, 121
plastromancy, 22
Po hexagram, 132
potted plants, 20
progressed hexagram, 30, 95–97

**Q**
qi, 16–17, 18, 178–179
    flow of, 78
Qian hexagram, 110, 124
Qian trigram, 47–49
questions
    asking, 37
    aspects of, 41
    coin-casting method, 85
    formulating, 40–41
    heart, from, 38
    useful, 39

**S**
san cai, 25
Sheng hexagram, 155
*Shenmiwehnua*, 9
Shi He hexagram, 130
Shi hexagram, 116
sixty-four hexagrams, 29, 104–177
social interactions, 78–79
Song hexagram, 115
space
    clearing, 36
    ritual in, 42

spiritual, interaction with, 178–183
Sui hexagram, 126
Sun hexagram, 150
synchronicity, 10

**T**
Ta Chuan, 29
tai chi, 18
Tai hexagram, 120
tantien, 37
Tao, 10
Taoism, 10
Taoist philosophy, 8, 32, 45
Thunder, 27
Thunder trigram, 55–57
Tong Ren hexagram, 122
tortoises, 22
    shell, 23
transformed hexagram, 95–97
trigrams, 22
    bottom line, 45
    eight, 25, 27, 44–79
    key to, 45
    middle line, 44
    origins of concept, 25–27
    social interactions and, 78–79
    three lines, 44–45
    top line, 44
trinity of heaven, earth, humanity, 26

**U**
Ultimate Beginning, 25
Ultimate Nothingness, 18
Universal Chart, 24
Universal Creative Order, 8
universal energy, 16–17
universal message, 11

**W**
Water, 17, 24, 27
Water trigram, 63–65
Wei Ji (Wei Chi) hexagram, 173
Wen Dang, Emperor, 9, 29
West Life Group, 179
Wind, 27
Wind trigram, 59–61
Wood, 24
Workbook exercises, 21, 31, 38, 43, 79, 85, 87,
    89, 96, 103
    answers to, 184
wu chi, 18
Wu Wang hexagram, 134

**X**
Xian (Hsien) hexagram, 140
Xiao Guo (Hsaio Kuo) hexagram, 171
Xiao Xu hexagram, 118
Xu hexagram, 114
Xun (Sun) hexagram, 166
Xun trigram, 59–61

**Y**
Yi hexagram, 136, 151
yin and yang, 18, 25, 78, 179
    balanced combination, 18
    study of change, 19–20
ying, 10
Yu hexagram, 125

**Z**
Zhen (Chen) hexagram, 160
Zhen trigram, 55–57
zhi gua, 30, 95–97
Zhong Fu (Chung Fu) hexagram, 170
Zhun hexagram, 112

# QUICK REFERENCE GUIDE

| LOWER TRIGRAM \ UPPER TRIGRAM | HEAVEN | EARTH | THUNDER | WIND | WATER | FIRE | MOUNTAIN | LAKE |
|---|---|---|---|---|---|---|---|---|
| **HEAVEN** | 1 Qian page 110 | 11 Tai page 120 | 34 Da Zhuang page 143 | 9 Xiao Xu page 118 | 5 Xu page 114 | 14 Da You page 123 | 26 Da Xu page 135 | 43 Guai page 152 |
| **EARTH** | 12 Pi page 121 | 2 Kun page 111 | 16 Yu page 125 | 20 Guan page 129 | 8 Bi page 117 | 35 Jing (Chin) page 144 | 23 Po page 132 | 45 Cui page 154 |
| **THUNDER** | 25 Wu Wang page 134 | 24 Fu page 133 | 51 Zhen page 160 | 42 Yi page 151 | 3 Zhun page 112 | 21 Shi He page 130 | 27 Yi page 136 | 17 Sui page 126 |
| **WIND** | 44 Gou page 153 | 46 Sheng page 155 | 32 Heng page 141 | 57 Xun page 166 | 48 Jing (Ching) page 157 | 50 Ding page 159 | 18 Gu page 127 | 28 Da Guo page 137 |
| **WATER** | 6 Song page 115 | 7 Shi page 116 | 40 Jie page 149 | 59 Huan page 168 | 29 Kan page 138 | 64 Wei Ji page 173 | 4 Meng page 113 | 47 Kun page 156 |
| **FIRE** | 13 Tong Ren page 122 | 36 Ming Yi page 145 | 55 Feng page 164 | 37 Jia Ren page 146 | 63 Ji Ji page 172 | 30 Li page 139 | 22 Bi page 131 | 49 Ge page 158 |
| **MOUNTAIN** | 33 Dun page 142 | 15 Qian page 124 | 62 Xiao Guo page 171 | 53 Jian (Chien) page 162 | 39 Jian (Chen) page 148 | 56 Lu page 165 | 52 Gen page161 | 31 Xian page 140 |
| **LAKE** | 10 Lu page 119 | 19 Lin page 128 | 54 Gui Mei page 163 | 61 Zhong Fu page 170 | 60 Jie page 169 | 38 Kui page 147 | 41 Sun page 150 | 58 Dui page 167 |